DEATH

Peter Mullen left ... time truanting – ... and warehouses ... Statistics Department of the Ministry of Labour before reading Philosophy and Psychology as a mature student at Liverpool University. Ordained in 1970, from 1977 he has been a country parson; he is currently Vicar of Tockwith and Bilton with Bickerton in the Diocese of York. He is the author of several books including *Being Saved* and *The New Babel*, is an experienced radio and television broadcaster, and writes and reviews for the *Daily Mail*.

DEATH
BE NOT PROUD

PETER MULLEN

Collins
FOUNT PAPERBACKS

First published in Great Britain by
Fount Paperbacks, London in 1989

Copyright © Peter Mullen 1989

Printed and bound in Great Britain by
William Collins Sons & Co. Ltd, Glasgow

In memory of my father
JAMES WALTER MULLEN
departed this life 5 May 1987

As death, when we come to consider it closely, is the true goal of our existence, I have formed during the last few years such close relations with this best and truest friend of mankind, that this image is not only no longer terrifying to me, but is indeed very soothing and consoling! And I thank my God for graciously granting me the opportunity of learning that death is the *key* which unlocks the door to our true happiness. I never lie down at night without reflecting that – young as I am – I may not live to see another day. Yet no one of all my acquaintances could say that in company I am morose or disgruntled. For this blessing I daily thank my Creator and wish with all my heart that each one of my fellow-creatures could enjoy it.

Mozart to his father from Vienna
4th April 1787

(Mozart died in 1791, aged 35)

CONTENTS

ACKNOWLEDGEMENTS

The author and publishers are grateful for permission to use material from V. Scannell: *New and Collected Poems* (Robson Books); T. S. Eliot: *Collected Poems and Plays* (Faber & Faber); T. Stoppard: *Rosencrantz and Guildenstern are Dead* (Faber & Faber); and E. Pound: *Collected Shorter Poems* (Faber & Faber).

PREFACE

Much modern philosophy and, indeed, ordinary secular chat, seems to assume that life is absurd and death is the end. I believe that these two judgements are, in different ways, erroneous and shallow. They do not do justice to the richness of human experience and to all the great words, pictures and music of our civilization. Those judgements are antihuman, negative and stultifying.

They are also unbiblical.

In this book I have gone back to the Bible and to the Prayer Book – as well as to the poetry, pictures and music of our tradition – and looked again at what is said there about life and death.

In doing so, I have not felt myself to be involved in a gloomy or morbid task. On the contrary, I have been much encouraged and reassured. I offer this book in the hope that others too may be similarly encouraged.

PETER MULLEN

1

The Fear of Death

One summer day, when I was five years old, I was running down a cobbled street in Leeds with two friends. It was, I remember, near the beginning of the long school holiday. Days and weeks of unimpeded enjoyment lay ahead. We were, as I said, only running over the cobbles; but even now I can feel in my memory the elation I felt at that moment. To call it Joy would not be an overstatement.

As we hurtled round the corner, we met another of our friends. He was sitting on the pavement, clutching a dirty handkerchief to his face, wailing at the top of his voice. We discovered the coal lorry had run over his dog. All that earlier elation evaporated. The blaze of July might have been a January fog. It was the first time that I can recall when I saw anyone else in utter misery. So I became miserable too. The puzzling thing was Why? Michael Hanson's dog had never been my dog. I had not even liked the dog much – Michael Hanson neither, if it came to that.

A little boy sitting on the pavement weeping because his dog had been killed. It was a regular, almost banal event. But I felt unrelievably sad. In grown-up words, it was like a true but brutal annunciation: Look, this is what the world is like! Somehow, on that sunny day in the back streets of Leeds not long after the war, I knew – without of course knowing how I knew, and without being able to express my feelings – that I had felt something deep and frightening. Deep because true; frightening because unavoidable. Grief and mortality. Twenty years later I came across T. S. Eliot's words in *Four Quartets*:

> . . . the backward half-look
> Over the shoulder, towards the primitive terror.
> Now, we come to discover that the moments of agony
> . . . are likewise permanent
> With such permanence as time has. We appreciate this
> better
> In the agony of others, nearly experienced,
> Involving ourselves, than in our own.[1]

Yes, that was exactly how I felt. It was not the fear of dying, of being run over even, like Michael's dog. It was not a fear of sickness or disease. It was something beyond any childish words I knew then. And it is only rarely conveyed even by the art of the best poets. It was the fear of death.

It was the apprehension of sorrow, permanent sorrow, in limited time – in "such permanence as time has". There were limits beyond which I was not allowed to go: the main road, the railway line and other boundaries. Now here was a boundary more fixed than all the others.

Such feelings of heaviness do not last long in the life of a small boy. By next morning, I had forgotten it, shrugged it off. And yet not quite. It no longer pressed upon me acutely, but it was always there, part of the scenery, a dark corner which one is obliged to visit from time to time. Or like a bad dream, banished by the daybreak, but requiring only some casual remark, some chance association, to bring back to mind its full horror.

Three years later there was another accident involving a lorry. This time it was the truck which delivered the school milk. One of my school-pals had been doing what we were always being told not to do: hitching a ride on the back of the lorry as it crossed the schoolyard. He fell off and the truck, reversing, crushed him. The accident had happened before the start of morning school and so, as children came through the gate, we saw the tarpaulin covering our friend's body. There was the lorry with its half unladen crates of milk. And there was our Headmistress saying nothing but waving us all briskly into school.

No one spoke as we hurried through the door. I remember no more about the incident. Only that it was a cold, grey day. The tarpaulin and the policeman by the lorry. And the Headmistress with her handkerchief in one hand, the other hand kept in perpetual motion as she rushed us all past the scene.

Michael weeping over his dog. It was the same feeling:

... the backward half-look
Over the shoulder, towards the primitive terror.

This experience too contained sorrow, sadness at the loss of a friend. But it was more: there was, again, a certain atmosphere – I am not now limited by the vocabulary of an eight year old, and so I can call it what the Psalmist called it – The Shadow of Death. And this time the darkness was compounded by the fact – I had only to look at the Headmistress's face – that grown-ups were not immune.

On 6 February 1952 I was again in the playground. The whistle blew for the end of morning break and we all formed up in our lines. We had a Headmaster by this time, and he came out to speak to us. He was usually cheerful, not above joining in ball-games with children; but on this morning he looked severe. There in the playground only a hundred yards from the black castle, Armley Jail, he announced that King George VI had died at Sandringham. It was one of those winter days when it barely lightened. The sky was solid, not so much grey as yellow. After the announcement, we stood in silence for a minute or so, and I remember the town hall clock booming eleven.

Here was death again. Puzzling. Unsettling. Even kings must die. That yellow sky seemed to be a sign, somehow. These feelings, I believe, are universal. That is why we know very well what Shakespeare means when he says:

> When beggars die, there are no comets seen;
> The heavens themselves blaze forth the death of
>   princes.[2]

All that day I was uneasy. What I felt then, I would now describe as depression perhaps. It was an anxious, heavy feeling. Something important had gone forever. And it had been taken away by precisely that thing which itself would never go away: death, the knowledge of death, the certainty of death and hence the fear of death.

That winter night, by the fireside and with the curtains drawn, I asked my parents what happens when we die. They told me that, of course, we go to heaven. Heaven is where God, Jesus and the angels are. So why did not this shining promise assuage the fear of death? Why does it not do so still?

These feelings are not, I must stress again, uppermost in a young lad's mind. I was not a morbid, sickly child – no precocious pre-Raphaelite, pale-faced and "half in love with easeful death". My chief concerns were cricket and football – both the playing of these games and the keeping – in the manner of little boys – of copious records. But my experience of death had set my life in a new context, in a larger room, from which there was no escape.

One of my aunts died and my parents with my mother's

brother returned in unfamiliar black clothes from the snowy funeral in New Wortley Cemetery. Uncle's sadness, and the way he held me more tightly before he left that night. In Sunday School, these issues were being talked about more formally. *When I survey the wondrous cross, on which the Prince of Glory died.* Good Friday and hot-cross buns. I believed that Jesus rose from the dead. But, like heaven itself, that did not take away the anxiety. Easter eggs. Daffodils. The walk to Emmaus. *All in the April evening.* It was a good story, and true, no doubt. But the valley of the shadow was truer.

The first really "close" death occurred when I was eleven. It was preceded by an odd experience to which I do not attach any supernatural significance but which is of a sort I have received perhaps half a dozen times since. I set it down now simply because it was a part of the whole event of my grandma's death – or at least it was part of what that death meant to me, how I felt it.

Grandad and Grandma had a newsagent's shop where I used to spend a lot of time reading all the comics and children's papers, free of charge. Grandma used to mind the shop while Grandad was out delivering the papers. When trade was slack, she would sit on a chair in the living-room and look into the shop from there in case a customer should appear. She was sitting there one Friday evening in October 1953 when I set off for my own house. As I stepped out of the shop on to the pavement, I turned and called goodbye to my Grandma. She waved. A voice – not a voice you could hear, but words inside the head – abruptly and blandly said: "You won't see your Grandma again." Next morning she died.

To the apprehension of death was added more strangeness. And now there was the fear of ghosts. I hated to go upstairs to the lavatory by myself. I was "seeing"

Grandma – or fearful of seeing her – everywhere. In time, and after more deaths, the intense sense of being haunted wore off, as these things do. I sometimes think it is a necessary part of coping with the world, as we starkly experience it as adults, that we become less sensitive to these atmospheres than we were as children. It remains true that those childhood experiences – both joy and horror, Christmas Eve *and* the tarpaulin in the playground – are formative. They are always with us. And any search for meaning in life – I do not mean philosophical or metaphysical meaning but individual, personal sense – will have to begin with them. "You must become as a little child." And, "We die with the dying, we are born with the dead."

What we experience is not objective time, sixty seconds in a minute, sixty minutes in the hour and so on. If we are doing something we enjoy, time races. If we are alone and awake in the night, it drags. When we are children time passes slowly and we remember even now how slowly it passed: the endless sunny summers, the eternity that it seemed to take for us to move from, say, Class Two to Class Three. This is partly because time is measured by how much we have experienced. It could not be – as felt time – measured by anything else. Three months of summer is a big proportion of the life of a five-year-old. And so that same three months period seems much longer to a child than to a forty-year-old.

It is the spaciousness of time which helps keep the child in the illusion of eternity. He thinks he will live forever. Or, rather, he does not positively discuss the issue with himself. It is a kind of unuttered assumption. Only when experiences of death, such as I have mentioned, arise does the child receive his first intimations of mortality. The awareness of death, that he is not on earth

16

forever, is disturbing. It is this new awareness – which amounts to nothing less than a new vision of reality – which provokes nightmares and other anxieties in the ordinary life of the child.

The acquisition of knowledge, as the two trees in the Garden of Eden demonstrate, is at once the dawning consciousness of sex and death. These two aspects of human experience are not merely unavoidable but, as Freud taught us, they are also inseparable. The awareness of death, not as an abstract idea but as a personal certainty – I shall die one day – is traumatic. It is a life's work to get used to the truth of it.

But why is death feared? Why are ghosts terrifying and the grave macabre? We accept our birth, why can we not so readily accept our death? The following are only a few suggested answers to these imponderable issues.

Death is feared because it is not our first or natural expectation. The young child, until he is taught otherwise – often by cruel experience – imagines himself immortal. The myths, legends and fairytales of our civilization bear this out: how often they begin with the hero, carefree, a bright, sunny day stretching out before him. This is the allegory of his innocence. It is the same with Adam and Eve in the paradise garden: knowledge includes knowledge of death. Before they eat of the fruit of the tree, they are innocent.

Then perhaps we are the only creatures on earth who have an intellectual apprehension of death as something that will happen to "me". No doubt many other animals, nearing death, have some sort of instinct about what is to occur, or even some imprinted behaviour pattern. But man alone is able, in the full flush of health and at the height of his powers, to know in language that one day he will die. As Socrates said, "All men are mortal." And we know it. This produces anxiety, firstly because it is knowledge we can do nothing about, and secondly because it is paradoxical knowledge: we know we shall die, but we do not know what death is. What we know is also what we do not know. As St John put it: "What we are, we know. What we shall be, it doth not yet appear."[3]

The fear of death must be distinguished from the fear of dying. None of us desires an agonizing death, and perhaps we greatly fear it. But that is not what is meant by the fear of death. The Psalmist – to whom, it seems, belong all the great psychological insights – fears death because it is an event which leaves him "cut off"; "gone hence and no more seen"; "gone down to the pit". He fears, "Not being had in remembrance."

In modern jargon we should probably express these fears in terms of "ego extinction". It all amounts to the same thing: a horror at the fact that time will proceed and we shall no longer be a part of it. Is that all there is to it, our egotism? Not quite, for our unwillingness to be excluded from time and flux is compounded by our ignorance of what constitutes the exclusion. Shakespeare, more eloquently than the rest of us, but describing a feeling we have all felt, says that death may be "a consummation devoutly to be wished" and "by a sleep to say we end the heartache and the thousand natural shocks". He even considers that the pains of existence might be ended by the act of suicide. We could our "quietus make with a bare bodkin".

However, we do not and cannot know that death is no more than an eternal sleep, a permanent quietus:

> To die, to sleep;
> To sleep: perchance to dream: ay, there's the rub.
> For in that sleep of death what dreams may come

18

When we have shuffled off this mortal coil,
Must give us pause.[4]

Shakespeare's language manages to catch and exhibit what lies at the bounds of sense and intelligence: the truth that we cannot imagine ourselves not being and yet we know that death is certain. Tom Stoppard, rewriting *Hamlet* in *Rosencrantz and Guildenstern are Dead*, fences with the same problem:

ROS: . . .Do you ever think of yourself as actually *dead*, lying in a box with a lid on it?

GUIL: No.

ROS: Nor do I, really . . . It's silly to be depressed by it. I mean one thinks of it like being *alive* in a box, one keeps forgetting to take into account the fact that one is *dead* . . . which should make a difference . . . shouldn't it? I mean, you'd never *know* you were in a box, would you? It would be just like being *asleep* in a box. Not that I'd like to sleep in a box, mind you, not without any air – you'd wake up dead, for a start and then where would you be? Apart from inside a box. That's the bit I don't like, frankly. That's why I don't think of it . . .

(GUIL. *stirs restlessly, pulling his cloak round him.*)

Because you'd be helpless, wouldn't you? Stuffed in a box like that, I mean you'd be in there for ever. Even taking into account the fact that you're dead, really . . . *ask* yourself, if I asked you straight off – I'm going to stuff you in this box now, would you rather be alive or dead? Naturally, you'd prefer to be alive. Life in a box is better than no life at all. I expect. You'd have a chance at least. You could lie there thinking – well, at least I'm not dead! In a minute someone's going to bang on the lid and tell me to come out. (*Banging on the floor with his fists.*) 'Hey you, whatsyername! Come out of there!'

GUIL.: (*Jumps up savagely*) You don't have to flog it to death![5]

Death is not exactly "the unknown". It is partially known and that is what makes us uneasy about it. We do not know what happens to us after death, and that is a worrying thought. Yet we know enough about what goes on at the deathbed, of undertakers and shrouds, the parson, mournful words, and cold ground and the sickly delicateness of the crematorium. And this is enough to appal me. Must I face these things? Yes, there is no alternative.

It is the mixture of what is known with what is unknown that makes our apprehension of death shadowy, ghostly. And fear of ghosts is part of the fear of death. The idea that we might ourselves become ghosts is not encouraging. Worse still is the thought that those who were once so close to us might even now be living some ghostly existence. This thought plunges us again into uncertainty. We think death is final – surely that is what "death" means – but perhaps there are revenants? This is unsettling and always gives rise to a sense of the macabre. Not for nothing have most cultures and civilizations elaborated ritual ways of dealing with departed spirits. In Christianity these are traditionally the funeral and the Requiem, the threefold laying to rest:

Rest eternal grant unto them O Lord
And let light perpetual shine upon them.

O Lamb of God that takest away the sins of the world
Have mercy upon us, grant us thy peace.

The emphasis is on a God-given finality, a laying to rest which is done by the mourners but done also by the Other World.

Sex and death inseparable, and guilt surrounding them both. So with the idea of death comes the idea of judgement and fear multiplied: for "we have left undone those things which we ought to have done" and "done those things which we ought not to have done". "And there is no health in us" – i.e. we are dead. It does not matter whether we believe literally in a judgement which will take place after death; it is simply that death, being irrevocable, is the sign par excellence of imperfection. And we fear the ghosts of others because these remind us of the ill we did to them (and the good we did not do to them) while they were alive. Ghosts visit, or seem to us to visit, the condemnation of eternity upon us while we ourselves are still prisoners of time. The judgement of eternity cannot be avoided, as death cannot be avoided: there is the final terror of the parable of the Sheep and the Goats.

Worse than all these perhaps is the way in which the fact of our death makes us question our personal worth, and so all worth, all value. We know we must die, and so, in a sense, we transcend our death. But still we must die. This may strike us as outrageous. (Indeed, outrage is one of the first and strongest reactions to bereavement, and I shall discuss it in a later chapter.) It does not seem fair to us that creatures who can apprehend their own death, and so rise above the brute fact of it, should, after all, be forced to die. Why? The question of value and meaning in life. One overpowering sensation, occurring to many, is that the world is meaningless and our lives are meaningless: "it is a tale told by an idiot, full of sound and fury, signifying nothing."[6]

The doctrine of the world's meaninglessness is not merely a doctrine, something held with the cold force of logical compulsion. It is a feeling of an overpowering sense of futility. In our own time many writers have presented this sensation, described it for us, sometimes in a very few words, or in a telling phrase. So Albert Camus writes of life's fundamental absurdity. It is as if one should roll a boulder up a hill only to watch it roll back down, then to have to roll it up again: the myth of Sisyphus, or life as cutting the grass. Martin Heidegger speaks of mankind as coming into the world without choice (which is certainly true), of our existence as inauthentic, and our condition as people "Thrown in". The feeling of meaninglessness and absurdity can lead to anxiety (angst), a daily terror or aching worry that will not go away: Sartre calls this "Nausea". It is the sickness unto death.

There is a fashion for thinking that the sense of the absurd, of meaninglessness is new to our time. This is not true. The Psalmist knows despair: "Out of the deep have I called unto thee, O Lord" and "My God, my God, why hast thou forsaken me?" The chief sin in the monasteries, houses of prayer in the age of faith, was accidie – ennui, listlessness, or the overriding sense of futility.

The sense of life's absurdity is nothing to do with particular inconveniences, such as that I did not get that promotion, or that I was unlucky in love. The meaninglessness under discussion here is of an all-embracing kind. *Whatever* happens has no purpose – it cannot make me feel that life makes any sense. You make a million pounds: so what? You marry Helen of Troy: so what? Nothing matters. All experience provokes the one response: so what?

And the reason why nothing matters? Because of our perpetual awareness of death, before which all riches, all relationships must pall. We are born with the potential for becoming aware of our own death, and, in due course, we do become so aware. It seems a cheat. We could feel we were eternal, because our intellect can contain death. Yet we must die. Or as Scripture puts it, we are made a little lower than the angels . . . and yet all things living come to nought. Shakespeare says, "Golden lads and girls all must, as chimney-sweepers, come to dust."[7]

"Man that is born of a woman hath but a short time to live, and is full of misery." These words from the Prayer Book are not talking about the misery of poverty or misfortune in business. It is a reference to accidie, to the sense of futility, angst, inauthentic existence and nausea which is referred to elsewhere as "the valley of the shadow". "He cometh up, and is cut down, like a flower; . . . and never continueth in one stay." These noble words are not mere descriptions of fact. In that rhythm, in *The Burial of the Dead*, they are said regretfully. Would that reality was otherwise. Even, suggests Scripture, it was once. In paradise. Before the dark dawning consciousness of death – the pestilence that walketh in darkness and the sickness that destroyeth in the noonday. Before I saw Michael Hanson weeping over a dead dog.

Not everyone feels the fear of death so acutely. There are individual differences here as everywhere else. But from time to time each one of us becomes suddenly conscious of our finite nature: it may be by an illness, the death of a relative or even a newspaper account of a road accident.

Our awareness of death sets us in a peculiar relationship with time. We feel the passage of time and, because we know it goes in only one direction, we try to grab hold of it. Even if we do not believe we can halt its progress, we do at least attempt to mark it with birthdays, anniversaries and other celebrations that are part of life's ritual. In an age of faith, the feasts and fasts of the Church's year were such landmarks, and their eternal return was some sort of comfort – just as springtime (and Easter) were celebrations of life in the face of death.

Anniversaries and festivals evoke a quality which is powerful in our attempt to cope with the awareness of death: nostalgia. We take photographs. We reminisce. We invest particular times with extra meaning and significance and so seek to cling to the passing moment.

The subverting of death is a common pursuit among the great artists. Mahler asked, "Why do we live? Why do we suffer? Is all this a great horrible jest? We must answer these questions if we are to go on living, if we are only to go on dying." Every one of his symphonies contains a funeral march. T. S. Eliot turns death and the deceitful flux of time into great poetry – great because it helps us cope with the fact of death. *Four Quartets* resonate with death's drum and with a poetic, human consciousness which seeks to rise above mere mortality. You might say that the whole artistic enterprise is an attempt to subvert death, "to leave", as Samuel Beckett said, "a stain on the silence".

Some of Eliot's words strive to do this:

In my beginning is my end. In succession
Houses rise and fall, crumble, are extended, . . .

24

Time and the bell have buried the day, . . .

What is the late November doing
With the disturbance of the spring?

O dark, dark, dark. They all go into the dark,
The vacant interstellar spaces, the vacant into the
     vacant
. . . all go into the dark.

Midwinter spring in its own season
Sempiternal though sodden towards sundown,
Suspended in time . . .[8]

The nostalgia is tangible, potent, just as it is in
Mahler's music, in Elgar, or Dennis Potter's television
plays *Pennies from Heaven* and *The Singing Detective*: the
willed organization of nostalgia as an antidote to the
threat of death. I shall try to say more about this in the
chapter which ends this book. Nostalgia and what Noel
Coward called "the potency of cheap music" – these are
the weapons with which we seek to fend off the last enemy.

Am I perhaps laying it on a bit thick? We know we must
die, but most of us do not, after all, spend our lives in
terrified or depressed contemplation of the fact. True,
and I would argue that our resolute cheerfulness is more
than a tribute to human heroism. We continue to behave
as if we are immortal. We make absolute rules and
create, in every aspect of life, standards. We fly in the face
of death.

Yet death and the consciousness of it re-emerge in our
greatest creations. The quintessence of drama is the
tragedy. Our noblest music is the Requiem and settings
of Christ's passion. Christ's passion is itself the story of

25

our passion. We retell the story that he did not deserve to die, and the story is felt because we do not believe that we deserve to die.

Why? Why should it be like this? We have a consciousness of infinity. We tell stories about the immortal gods – we who must die. We sing songs about the old days and hope thereby mystically to turn back the clock. And nostalgically, as we sing, the clock seems to be turned back: "We are the music while the music lasts."

Though our lives are haunted, we can turn our anxiety into artistic creations of great beauty. And even finite existence, lives which are lived in the knowledge that they will come to an end, can subvert death and morally and spiritually triumph over death by being lives of unselfishness, service, purposefulness and love.

2

The Distinguished Thing –
The Experience of Death

"So here it is at last, the distinguished thing," was a sentence which Henry James seemed to hear, in his own voice, when he was falling due to a stroke. "Distinguished" in the paradoxical sense that, while death is commonplace, each person's death is unique. Distinguished too in the sense that this thing, death, is what the whole of life has been leading up to; this thing in anticipation of which we have lived.

In twenty years as a parish priest, I have observed many deaths. And yet, in the majority of cases, "observed" is not the right word: every priest and pastor knows the privilege and pain of being involved in the experiences of the dying parishioner. These experiences are various, but there are broad similarities in the range of reactions to the imminent prospect of death.

I shall tell the story of one man's last months. While this is obviously the story of a particular and unique person, his developing attitude towards death is common enough.

"John", as I shall call him, was reasonably well-off, a successful businessman in his late fifties. I had visited him a few years earlier when he was being treated for cancer of the bowel. After an operation which went well, he took early but active retirement. About three years later he felt some discomfort and so went to see the specialist. As he afterwards related to me, the conversation went something like this:

"Well, John, it's not good news I'm afraid."

"Has there been a progression of the cancer?"

"Yes. I'd hoped to have cured it completely in the operation, but . . . I'm sorry."

John wanted to know precisely how bad the "not good" news was. The doctor asked him if he really wanted him to be so explicit. Yes, he was quite sure.

"How long?"

"Three months – perhaps a little longer, but not much."

John was devastated. As he told me, "I thought he was going to give me a couple of years."

The disease was cancer of the liver and, at the time of the doctor's announcement, John did not actually look ill and his complaining had been only of "discomfort". This made the bad news all the more shocking. After the initial shock, his attitude was of disbelief. This is common. "Look, he's got it wrong. Doctors have been wrong before. I don't even feel ill!" I have heard these words many times. Sometimes the patient desperately asks for a second opinion.

After a week or so, John reluctantly concluded that the doctor was probably not wrong. And so his typical reaction entered its second phase: anger and outrage.

"Why me?"

This is the period when personal historical reflections, reflections which often include moral and spiritual speculations – "It's not as if I've abused my body . . . never been a heavy drinker . . . always eaten sensibly" –

develop into moral as well as physical self-justification – "I've tried to lead a good life, to do as I would be done by." This sort of moral reasoning often rises to theological heart-searching: "Why has God done this to me?" Frequently the sufferer affirms his lifelong belief in God – God who brought him home safely from the war, for instance. And he may assert, as John asserted, that to punish a believer by an untimely death from a disgusting disease is not fair play on God's part.

This attitude may persist. We have to face the fact that some people do die very unhappy, in bitterness, perplexity and disillusion. There may be sleepless, horrible nights and distressing emotional scenes. And the sufferer's pain is often compounded by a sense of guilt. For, while he may protest his moral uprightness and lifelong theological rectitude, it is often the case that he suspects he must have been "bad" in some way and that his "punishment" is perhaps justified. And will the punishment cease at death? Or is there hell to come? This is the stage in which theological propositions of a general sort are spoken. The dying person may even convey an attitude of disinterestedness: "What sort of God is it who allows evil and suffering in the world? It would have been better not to have created the world in the first place!" And the classic: "If God is omniscient, omnipotent and good – where does evil come from?"

However purely intellectual and abstract these reasonings appear, they are almost always rooted in the personal experience of suffering, shock and disillusion. I have watched theologians die and, strangely enough, these usually have been unforthcoming with theological speculations!

My parishioner, John, endured all these different stages and the distress that goes with them. Happily, he entered another state of mind, less painful and more constructive. Happily, too, his is a mood or disposition which many people achieve and it can be summed up in John's own words: "Well, I'm going to make the most of the time that's left!"

Sometimes this resolution can be very thoroughgoing and generate the hot flush of terminal vocation. In John's case it showed itself as a renewed urge to take and to process photographs. And he embarked on a diary of his doings and of his mental and spiritual state. Such determined activities may be carried on with great intensity and devotion. All imminent death – as with the prospect of being hanged, according to Dr Johnson – "concentrates his mind wonderfully".

The distinguished thing belongs to the experience of the parish priest or near relative, or anyone who regularly spends time with the dying man. The concentrated mind feels the reality of time strongly. Here, when we know time it strictly limited, we feel its passing intimately. There is a tangible sadness and regret in the fleeting moment. Minutes and seconds heavy, dew-laden, autumnal. These can be depressing. They may also be very moving – the raw material and origin of true spiritual awakening. This reassurance lies hidden in the apparent flippancy of Dr Johnson's saying about the concentrated mind.

If this constructive phase occurs in a final illness, it is the job of the priest, counsellor, friend or near relative to do all he can to encourage it. When the dying person's will is stirred to action, it is a moving experience for those near to him. It is, after all, life heroic in the face of death: going through the vale of misery and using it for a well. It is part of what is distinguished about the distinguished thing.

From a practical point of view, it is important to see that the sufferer does not overtax or overtire himself in his weakening state. And it is even more important to make sure that his psychological aims and expectations are not too high, for failure to come up to standards which he has set for himself will lead to the recurrence of depression and even despair. For the diarist, half a page each day, or merely a couple of sentences: he must not grow to believe it has fallen to him to write *War and Peace*.

Even in a constructive period, the dying person will have moments of relapse, of shock and panic. "My God, it really is happening to me! I'm the one who's dying!" This may erupt at any time, in any place. It is important never to leave him on his own for too long therefore. Let a comforting word, a cup of tea or whatever form reassurance best takes, be always on hand.

The dying person will desire to spend some of his time alone, but usually not much. The awareness of encroaching death often produces loneliness. This is in part caused by the fact of disease. The Biblical writers understood well enough that sickness is frequently associated with sin. The sufferer may feel unclean, not fit for human company. And this is especially true if the nature of his sufferings are embarrassing or alienating because of their appearance. There is not much to encourage fellow feeling in jaundice, nausea and incontinence. And these things do not help a man's natural feeling of guilt.

Moments of horror will occur, but there will also be moments of elation, even of exaltation. As another parishioner once said to me: "I know I haven't long left and I don't like the idea. But yesterday I was down by the river in the afternoon sun. The rhododendrons were out, and there were one or two fishermen still as portraits by the old mill. Suddenly, a voice, my own voice but not aloud (not quite) said: 'You're dying Jean, but it doesn't matter.'" This is a mystical state defined by the fourteenth-century writer Mother Julian and quoted by T. S. Eliot:

> Teach us to care and not to care
> Teach us to sit still.[1]

It is, "The apprehension of timelessness in time, the occupation of a saint."

But between the Highs and the Lows, life, though lived as an exaggeration of itself, will go on as before. There will be ordinary things to do: working and shopping, answering the telephone, filling in the forms which universal bureaucracy – itself a form of death – visits upon us. Some of these things will be, at times, resented: "Why do I have to do such a trivial thing, in my condition?" At other times, they will be clung to: "I know it's trivial, mowing the lawn – but this may be the last time I shall do it."

In the dying person the ordinary mood swings of life are exaggerated. The mind is concentrated. The distinguished thing approaches and bears witness to itself before it fully arrives. The dying man may wish to visit familiar scenes, places that have a personal significance for him. It is easy enough to volunteer to drive him to these places, harder to know how to cope with his reactions when you arrive. For he goes back to a country pub, to a remembered place which may not have changed with the years: but he has changed, grown weaker perhaps, lost (because of illness) the taste for his old-time favourite drink. The recollection – the nostalgia – which makes him want to return to an old and familiar place, does not always take into account new weaknesses, invalidity, decrepitude. The immediate comparison therefore of time present with time past can be frustrating and depressing. It is not always a good idea to take the dying man back to his former haunts. Though there is no golden rule. Sometimes the evoked nostalgia is beneficial. He comes away with a sense of a task performed. He leaves fortified by the power of happier memories. But it is not always so, and the priest or friend should beware: for the dying man, a nostalgic visit can be a disaster – an example of what G. K. Chesterton called the stretching of "the folly of our youth to be the shame of age".

The dying man has enough shame. He does not require any stretching of it.

> We die with the dying,
> We are born with the dead.[2]

There are no rules, hard and fast in the presence of the distinguished thing, except sensitivity. We must take care, infinite care. It is all so difficult. We must be sensitive to his moods but not so oversensitive as to indulge him and to sound patronizing. Yet what a tightrope! For sometimes, if we agree with what he says, he will interpret it as a species of patronizing. But if, in all rationality, we disagree he may claim that, "It's all right for you. You're not dying, are you!" The fact that, by his provocation of guilt in us, he does not assuage his own guilt, will not be lost on him – even if it is lost on us.

We are meant, as the New Testament says, to be good neighbours to one another. We should help each other in life. And the injunction to bear one another's burdens means we must help one another in death, in the valley of the shadow. We need to be helped to die as we need to be helped to live. We must have solidarity with one another even – especially – in dying.

This is not easy. We tend to avoid the dying as we also avoid the bereaved: they are an embarrassment to us and a reminder of what we would rather forget – our own mortality. And the dying person challenges our convictions about the value of life and the purpose of death. We are forced to face the question, Why?

This is how it was with John. When he had to take to his bed, I would visit him often and we would talk for hours. Often the conversation was directly religious and theological: why does God allow all the suffering which we must endure in this world? Or there were philosophical considerations such as whether we possess an immortal soul, and what does that mean? And whether there is an aspect of us which survives the death of the body. How can these things be?

The odd thing was, in all these talks with John and with others in a similar situation, that the questions of life and death, while they were fascinating, did not seem to matter in an ultimate sense. They were not the main thing about our talks. They are in any case – and whatever anyone, evangelist or atheist, might say – insoluble questions. We all have our opinions but no one can claim to know for certain. And, in any event, even our own opinions may change with the passage of time. The only certainty upon which everyone must agree is that death does not wait until we have formed our opinions about it: we are cut down like flowers and never continue in one stay.

No, the most important thing – what is most basic and real – in the relationship between the dying person and his friend, priest, counsellor or companion is the relationship itself. In these special, unique conversations we enter the solidarity of death. They are the most revealing conversations of all, because they tell us what our true values are. In a brief, casual meeting with a dying man it is possible to get by with a grin and a platitude, with technique. But in regular conversations, fancies must fly away and the reality of what is happening must be faced. This can be, and usually is, of great value to both concerned.

There is no technique. Technique is only technical, belonging to machines and all things mechanical. Death is not mechanical but personal. Nevertheless, there are simple guidelines. The dying person needs neither the preaching of the Evangelical Alliance nor of the National Secular Society. There is something obscene, because merely wordy, about preaching in the face of indubitable and unavoidable reality. It has the same artificiality as, say, stopping the kisses to write her a poem. What the dying person needs is not sermons or proof texts, or even refined philosophical atheism from the Stoic party. He needs, and usually wants, that human solidarity of which I have already spoken: the feeling that we are in this thing together: the close compliance of another human being. Can you give him this? Some day it may very likely be your bounden duty to do so.

The relationship is a sort of unconscious conspiracy in the face of death. Not that death will be outwitted. Death will have the last word. But whether that last word is heard and received as a word of consummation or despair depends upon the quality of the personal relationship. Here is at least part of the meaning of "Heaven" and "Hell" – this side of the grave.

Among the simple guidelines, it seems only right to say that the dying person should be allowed to choose the form which the conversations take. This does not mean that the friend should merely indulge him: indeed there will be times when he needs to be firm, even strict. For example, the dying person has a right to feel sorry for himself. But inordinate bouts of self-pity will not help him and he should be eased – or sometimes even jolted – out of them.

He will want to talk about the old days. This is tribute to the importance of nostalgia again: it is a way of accepting the passage of time and death, time's inevitability. It is also a way of expressing that individual transcendence over time. Time, and hence even death, are, as it were, put into some sort of perspective by the dying person as he reveals in his recollections and expectations that his mind is not limited by the tyranny of the present time: that moving prison of the ego. He can talk about the past and envisage the future. This gives him dignity in the face of relentless time's most powerful weapon: death. He must die, but he is not overwhelmed by death. Death is put into perspective. And the perspective is that of the dying person's total experience of life – experience which he has had and which, therefore, even death cannot deny him.

Nostalgia can be helpful, cathartic. Reliving the past can help him cope with the present and what is to come. There will be tears but these can be tears of triumph rather than fear. As he recollects his life, he places himself in it, in time, and so recounts his own significance: as Beckett said, he leaves "a stain on the silence". The reliving of joys improves his sense of personal worth, and the recollection of "things ill done and done to others' harm" eases his conscience. Though it should be stressed that no attempt is to be made to coerce a "confession" out of a dying person. The expression of joy or sorrow should be left to his own spontaneity.

In the face of death, as the mind is concentrated, the dying person and his friend will explore the things that each finds valuable in life. This happened with John and me, and I am happy for him that it did, and also grateful

– for those intimate conversations taught me the nature of the things that really matter to me. Imminent death forces us to cut our way through forests of trivia and rubbish and to rediscover what we find important, what can really nourish us. These things are not always, or even generally, terrifically highbrow. John and I read and recited poetry and listened to some Mozart, Bach and Elgar; but we also had vivid and satisfying recollections of great innings for England and of that day when Jim Laker took nineteen wickets at Old Trafford. Of the Coronation and a day which, by coincidence and in different parts of the country, we both went fishing in the pouring rain and caught nothing. In fact, it is almost as if the more trivial the recollection the more significance it has: and this for the reason that life is more truly felt when it is rooted in the ordinary than in what is extraordinary.

Words are not the whole story. Even prayers are not the main thing in this relationship – though I have noticed that the most "felt" prayers – the ones which do the dying man the most palpable good – are likely to be prayers for others rather than expressions of supplication for his own condition. This is an aspect of the distinguishedness of the distinguished thing: it seems sometimes to confer grace on others. A dying man's prayers, not for himself but for another human being, are special. His loving, charitable recollections of others share the same quality.

Words fail – though that is not to denigrate them. Actions – though words are themselves a unique sort of action – speak louder. As the dying person approaches death, there are little acts that can be done for him. And our solidarity in life as in death confers upon humble actions a kind of simple grandeur and makes what is banal, or even distasteful, something of dignity. Give him a drink or clean him up. "Inasmuch as ye have done this to the least of these my little ones, ye have done it unto me." And we find we have. I do not wish to romanticize what is euphemistically called "terminal care". I have seen too much of it to want to do that. It can be a chore and a cause of anxiety. But there is something of the nature of what is sacramental about the giving of a drink, the plumping of a pillow, the fetching and carrying of bedpans. We are of the earth, earthy. If we can make no sense of earthly things, we shall get nowhere at all in our windy talk of heaven and things eternal.

C. G. Jung said that the first part of life is a journey outwards and the second part is a journey home. This means that, as we learn how to make our way in the world, we must also learn how to leave it. We must prepare for death, learn to die. This is not a matter of settling on philosophical answers to imponderable questions about the meaning of life or the nature of the hereafter – if any. It is a case of fulfilling our vocation, everyone's vocation, to learn to die as we learn to live. And if we have lived well we shall die well: that is the root of morality.

I do not mean to emphasize a strict moral code, but an acceptance of life, a little forbearance, kindness, warm-heartedness . . . and humour in the face of tribulation. Some of the strictest moralizers are singularly lacking in these mature, human qualities. Those who resent life and find it only a battle or a chore, who always see themselves as thwarted, as having been dealt a lousy hand – they will not find that the acceptance of death comes easily. We must learn to be kinder to ourselves. Not self-indulgent, but genuinely kind, loving ourselves: for it is love which helps us overcome our faults, binds up our wounds and, as the New Testament says, "covers a multitude of sins". Love your neighbour as yourself. Yes, and that involves loving yourself which is the hardest thing.

And yet it is the one thing necessary. True love seeks not to indulge the beloved or to pander, but to do precisely and only those things that will really benefit the beloved. It is the same with one's self. You must get to know yourself as you would wish to know any other beloved. You are your own soulmate. You must discover your character and what your deep, genuine needs are. Not diversions but needs. Then you must set about providing those needs. And when you find flaws and ugly patches, you must deal effectively and kindly with them, as you would with anyone else whom you love.

Encourage yourself by talking to yourself, aloud if you want to. It is not a sign of madness! When you talk to yourself you are talking to God – for the Kingdom of God is within you. This sort of warmheartedness is necessary to the living of a happy life. It is what the New Testament calls *agapē*, charity, true love. It is not only "the chiefest of virtues" but probably the only one. And it is not soppy or sentimental: The fires of love burn with a fiercer heat than the fires of hell, and that is why "death is swallowed up in victory". Charity shines a clear, searching light into all the corners, especially the dark corners, of our character; and it heals, forgives, redeems. Without it we are dead already.

Nothing can overcome charity for it bears all things. Charity is the one thing that can make us whole. It is the true perception and acceptance. It issues true from the redeemed part of ourself and redeems all the rest. It is like cancer in reverse. Encourage the charitable part, the warmhearted part of yourself and that part, that encouragement, will spread throughout your character. You will see things clearly. You will be filled with a happiness which nothing can take away from you. You will know as you are known. This is what redemption means: the clear burning light of love and all the scars healed.

This is true on the cosmic scale. It is the world's destiny. It is psychologically and spiritually true in each individual life. It is the one perfect truth. Not a philosophical or rationally derived truth. It is simply the only truth, indubitable, a felt, shared apprehension of enternal love. It is the goal of all our striving, the great consummation. Death is nothing in the face of it. Light, warmth, love:

> All shall be well
> And all manner of thing shall be well
> When the tongues of flame are infolded
> Into the crowned knot of fire
> And the fire and the rose are one.[3]

If we live like that, we shall die like that. And we shall help others to die. And they, by the same means, will help us. The rhythm of warmheartedness is the eternal dance of God. Because "No man is an island" and "Any man's death diminishes me" it is impossible to talk realistically about the death of another human being without at the same time reflecting on my own death. What the priest or friend does to help the dying man is only a form of what he must do as he considers and approaches his own death.

It is our duty, as far as within us lies, "to live in love and peace with all men". If we are given knowledge of our death as imminent or soon, it is a good thing to search out anyone with whom we are at odds and to try to end the quarrel. This is part of preparing what D. H. Lawrence called our "little ship of death". It is as much a part of making your will as the decision about to which nephew you will leave the gold cuff-links.

The terrifying consciousness of death can be overcome. All that anxiety and dread which arises directly out of our awareness of death's inevitability can be assuaged. For it is as natural to die as it is to be born. The natural forces are therefore finally on our side, working in our favour; only, as Jung said, we must learn how to avail ourselves of them. This is the journey home. The end and purpose of this journey is not death as an event but the acceptance of death.

This means we must face death for what it is – the mysterious stranger, the distinguished thing. St Francis came, by means of the love of all created things, to refer to "Our Sister death". This is the aim, warmhearted acceptance. It is not a case of bracing ourselves before a nasty shock, but of calmly welcoming this last and inevitable gift. The terrors of death are nothing compared to the terrors we should have to endure at the prospect of this life going on forever.

It is encouraging to see that many, even most, people do achieve a measure of acceptance. Don't worry and strain yourself seeking total acceptance. Perhaps God does not intend you for a saint. A little acceptance will go a long way. The rest will follow. I used to wonder why old people did not go mad. If you are eighty-five, life can seem to be rather one-directional. But it is children and young people who are most afraid of death. So how encouraging it is to see that, as we live, we do make progress in the vocation towards an acceptance of death. In the faces of many old people, this acceptance can be clearly seen. Sadly, in others there is only bitterness and despair. It is the difference between heaven and hell. Mozart died screaming; Mahler died with the name "Mozart" on his lips. John died peacefully, with a measure of acceptance, with his family and friends around him. It is a decent destiny: to leave life with a sense of gratitude for what is now past. The philosopher Wittgenstein died soon after he had said, "Tell them [his friends] I've had a good life." One of those friends, Norman Malcolm, wrote: "When I think of his profound pessimism, the intensity of his mental and moral suffering, the relentless way in which he drove his intellect, his need for love together with the harshness that repelled love, I am inclined to believe that his life was fiercely unhappy. Yet at the end he himself exclaimed that it had been 'wonderful!' To me this seems a mysterious and strangely moving utterance."[4]

There are less portentous but equally human deathbed scenes. I had a friend who was a High Court Judge. When I first came into the parish he telephoned to ask me over for a drink and I soon discovered that part of his motivation was to see what the Vicar looked like tipsy. He was a man with an enormous reputation for generosity – and an equal propensity for strong drink. As befits a Judge, he was highly intelligent but also sensitive and warmhearted: qualities he spiced with a mischievous sense of fun.

During the Judge's last illness, another friend was in the habit of taking his wife to fetch the weekly shopping. Once, upon their return, the Judge called out from his bed upstairs "Is that you, Michael? Is that you, Sally?" They went to join him. "Pour yourself a drink, Michael. And pour Sally one. Pour one for me while you're at it." Then he raised his glass, said, "Last orders!" and died. There are many worse ways to go, and moods to go in.

Life is unequal and so is death. Some people have a great fear of death while others seem naturally to accept it as part of the normal order of things. A religious faith may help, but then it depends what we mean by a religious faith. A neurotic preoccupation with "being

42

saved" or a tendency to appear as on nodding terms with the Almighty or the Lord Jesus Christ are not such sound preparation for death as that much deeper thing, the acceptance of life itself. If you are at odds with life, you will be at odds with death. And any religious faith worthy of the name must say at least as much about how to live in this world as about the life of the world to come. It is worth repeating to ourselves five times a day that:

> The first man is of the earth, earthy: the second man
> is the Lord from heaven . . . And as we have borne
> the image of the earthy, we shall also bear the image
> of the heavenly.[5]

That is the correct sequence: earth first, heaven later. And part of our earthiness is to suffer pain. This is one of the most distressing aspects of a long illness and a lingering death. We do not understand the mystery of suffering. Christians affirm that all suffering is part of the suffering of Christ and therefore redemptive. But that can sound merely glib in the face of an actual agony. Drugs can reduce or remove pain, and we are thankful for this fact as for the hospice movement and for more enlightened care of the dying. Hospital Staff in the old days would never officially admit that a patient was dying: it was regarded as a failure of medical science and nursing care. Nowadays the dying person is helped to die peacefully.

I knew an old lady who died a slow death in great pain. She did not talk about the pain much, but she asked continually about other parishioners and friends. She was not spectacularly religious in any obvious way: Church once a month perhaps, and she liked the whist-drive and the over-sixties trips to the Yorkshire coast, the cakes she bought at the Garden Party. Not obviously religious. But she had so lived, warmheartedly, that her concern for friends and neighbours was natural and real. This concern was more important to her than her pain. Pain she had, but, as she once said to me, "I'm not going to spend any time on it." Not obviously religious. I believe she was a saint. Her lack of self-preoccupation even in intolerable circumstances must be part of what is meant by the redemptive power of suffering.

Acceptance of death is never absolute. Even in the words of Christ from the cross there is ambiguity, psychological-spiritual aspects in ultimate opposition: "My God, my God, why hast Thou forsaken me?" *and* "Into Thy hands I commend my spirit."

Aim at a little acceptance. You cannot contrive to become a saint.

3

The Ritual of Disposal

Most deaths used to occur at home. The undertaker, usually a well-known member of the local community, would be sent for as readily as the doctor. As soon as the doctor had certified the death, the undertaker would wash and lay out the corpse and place it in its coffin. There was a tradition of viewing the body: friends and relations from near and far would come and "pay their respects".

Where I grew up, in the working-class industrial suburbs of Leeds, the coffin was set out in the best room – usually called "the front room" – which nearly always housed an upright piano (invariably out of tune) and an aspidistra (which had always "seen better days").

These front rooms were rarely used, except for laying-out. People did not have money to spare for coal for more than the living room. They might put a fire in the front room at Christmas or when it was some notable anniversary, like a Silver Wedding. Consequently, the room was usually rather damp, and the yellowing keys of the out-of-tune piano, overhung by the faded aspidistra, gave the place just the sort of genteel-dilapidated melancholy that suited the laying-out of Uncle Fred or Auntie Florrie.

The aspidistra, the piano and the coffin: nature, art and religion all in one room. The faintly musty smell and the quiet relieved only by the ticking of a clock which – though rarely did anyone consult it – was wound every day: another quasi-religious, ritual act. It was a powerful atmosphere in which to grow up and to have one's first intimations of mortality. Dust and damp, nostalgia and the solipsistic chiming of an unwatched clock. In such an atmosphere, you knew that death was, as Henry James said, a "distinguished thing".

The phrases spoken by attendant mourners were clichés, but clichés ennobled by intensity of feeling and so elevated almost to the status of liturgy. They would say of the deceased, "She looks lovely", "She's so peaceful". The old music-hall coined jokes on these sombre little rituals: "By gum, Fred looks a lovely colour! That fortnight at Blackpool did him a world of good!" And laughing at these jokes became, in those old working-class communities, almost a part of the ritual of mourning.

You were invited, but not obliged, to view the corpse. There was an etiquette about this as well, and it was one usually extended to children: "D'you want to look at your Auntie Florrie?" And, if the child did not so wish, then she was schooled to say, "No thank you. I'd rather remember her as she was."

Undertakers were "characters" who would often spin out comic-macabre stories about bodies who sat up or groaned (or performed even more unmentionable minor acts) long after their decease had been pronounced. A local undertaker told me of how he had once been summoned to lay out an old girl of ninety. When he arrived in her bedroom, he thought he noticed her blink an eye. Mere imagination, he said to himself. But then the old girl sat up and asked him plainly if he were the milkman!

Death with its folklore. Death and its trappings unavoidable. All these signs and signals, linguistic and social conventions arising out of an experience that was local, made it certain that the growing child would regard death as a distinguished thing. It was mysterious and scary, but it was real. And the damp, the piano, the aspidistra and the clock gave it a context, which, however worrying, meant that you had a way of putting death in perspective: that perspective was the shared life of the local community.

The destruction of those old houses, and therefore of the old communities, accomplished by the planners of the 1950s and 1960s, was another kind of death. I remember the promises (threats?) of "slum-clearance" and of how we were all going to be "rehoused". Actually, we dreaded the prospect. We lacked certain sanitary sophistications which the world of today regards as necessary to life; but we did not think of ourselves as slum-dwellers. We knew all our neighbours by name, and there was real informal charity in those old communities: the quirky, the dirty and the mildly mad were not regarded as they are presently regarded – as suitable cases for treatment by the vulture-like social workers – but as members of the neighbourhood who, because they *were* members of the neighbourhood, were tolerated, integrated and cared for.

Our capacity to cope with metaphysical and spiritual problems, as with death and bereavement, is at least partly determined by the strength of local ties and all the informal rituals and jokes, superstitions and etiquette that create a folk-religion. All truly felt religion is folk-religion. No one believed a word that the parson or the minister said at the funeral about life everlasting. What mattered was that the ritual of disposal was done rightly, that, in the colloquial and powerful idiom, respects were paid. Uncle Fred, him dead. See him off with ham. It was a matter of pride bordering on liturgical exactitude that these things were done rightly and done well.

All this is not quite true. There were always one or two

families in those old communities who were more formally and explicitly religious. They may have been "big noises" at the chapel, or they might have fallen under the spell of some lurid evangelist, got themselves born again and joined the Four Square Gospel. The description of folk like this was usually that they had "gone barmy". They were tolerated nonetheless, and integrated into the communality of sense, as far as possible. The really important thing to grasp about this is that conspicuous formal religious activity which actually set you apart from the human community was rare precisely because the real community and its power to provide social and emotional support was so strong. The naive religious "commitment" of today's suburban charismatics is a mark of our separation and sectarianism, of the weakness of real community life. As I said, in those old communities, we knew everybody: Mr Silly at number five, Mrs Prim at number ten. All sorts and conditions of men. On our sanitized new private estates we sometimes do not know even our next door neighbour. Naturally enough, this is reflected in our social life and also in our attitudes towards death, in our rituals of disposal.

The breaking down of the old local communities has loosened our grip on life and so also on the way we handle death. There is more distance between us nowadays. And so there is bound to be more formality, more attenuation of experience into the realm of what is official and abstract. So now our rituals of disposal make the first priority the removal of the corpse from the community in which it abode when it was animated. Gone the piano with its yellowing keys, the aspidistra and the clock. In their place the stereo and the video and the computer. Vile bodies do not lie easily in this new ambience, and so they are carted off to the Palace of Euphemism known as the Chapel of Rest.

The emotional shift is profound. The aspidistra culture guaranteed that the funeral service, and, in particular, the words of committal, marked the parting between living and dead. There was a continuum between the death and the disposal – a period, two or three days, during which the loss could be gradually got used to. The corpse in the front room was still one of us, part of us, part of the community. Nowadays, the arrival of the undertaker with his stretcher and the removal of the corpse while it is still warm is the act of disposal. Viewings in the Chapel of Rest and turning up three days later for further euphemistic activity at the crematorium are sorts of embarrassed afterthoughts, willed epiphanies of socially rootless emotions.

None of this is the fault of Superintendents of crematoria or of Environmental Health Officers: it is simply a consequence of the destruction of an earlier way of life and of its replacement by something more rarefied and artificial. Science provides one of the reasons why we can no longer cope intimately with the trappings of death. For Science is god now. All our faith in Science is founded: to cure us when we are ill; to replace failing parts by transplantation or gadget; to render impotence fertile and even, by techniques of resuscitation and ventilation, to redefine death. So, when a real death comes, inevitably as it must, this looks like a defeat for Science. So we remove the evidence as soon as possible, and our funeral rites become tributes to Science – or to all that is left of Science after its failure – exercises in cleanliness and sterilization.

When Lazarus died, his friends said, "He stinketh." The Revised Standard Version of the Bible says, "There will be an odour." In the Municipal Crematorium there

will not even be an odour. Ashes to ashes, dust to dust
... But dust has as little place in our contemporary funeral
rites as it has in those new front rooms with their stereos,
videos and computers. Only remember the aspidistra.

In the old days, the undertakers could usually call upon
one or two women who "for decency" would help him
with the laying-out – especially of females. I cannot think
that the task was pleasant, but there was something
wholesome about it, something that reminded me, as a
boy, of the Holy Saturday story and the taking down from
the cross, the anointing and laying to rest in the sepulchre.
This still happens in some villages, but the urban and
suburban procedure is quite different. The corpse is now
usually injected with an embalming fluid which
scientifically restores Uncle Fred's Blackpool tan without
his having been forced to endure the pre-decease agony
of an actual visit to that resort.

Bodies are still buried, but the practice is becoming
rare. Graves are dug, usually five foot deep for a single
grave and six feet for a double – that is when another
member of the family is to be buried in the grave. And,
at the moment of writing, the average cost of this means
of disposal – including a service in church but not
including any monument or memorial erected on the
grave – is £600 in the north of England and somewhat
more in the south: which must indicate that the ties of
property and its price which bind us in life are not escaped
in death.

Most corpses are, of course, cremated. I visited the
crematorium in York when I was preparing this book and
all the staff there were most helpful. York is a city of
100,000 people and the crematorium serves it and the
villages round about to a distance of forty miles in the
easterly and northerly directions. In 1987, the latest year

for which final figures are available, York cremated 2,394 corpses: forty a week in summer, rising to sixty or more in winter.

There is a finality about cremation more radical than that involved in a burial. Evidence is destroyed when a body is cremated. This could provide a cover for foul play. And so, meticulous precautions are taken. The relatives of the deceased must apply (on "Form A") for cremation under the Cremation Acts of 1902 and 1952.

This form makes rigorous enquiries:

1 Are you an executor or the nearest surviving relative of the deceased?

2 If not, state
   (a) Your relationship to the deceased
   (b) The reason why the application is made by you and not by an executor or any nearer relative.

3 Have the near relatives of the deceased been informed of the proposed cremation?

4 Has any near relative of the deceased expressed any objection to the proposed cremation? If so, on what ground?

5 What was the date and hour of the death of the deceased?

6 What was the place where the deceased died? (Give address and say whether own residence, lodgings, hotel, hospital, nursing home, etc.)

7 Do you know or have you any reason to suspect that the death of the deceased

was due, directly or indirectly, to (a) violence; (b) poison; (c) privation or neglect?

8 Do you know any reason whatever for supposing that an examination of the remains of the deceased may be desirable?

9 Give name and address of the ordinary medical attendant of the deceased.

10 Give names and addresses of the medical practitioners who attended deceased during his or her last illness.

The undertaker must bring to the crematorium a Certificate to Cremate. He must also bring a set of cremation forms signed by a doctor and confirmed by a second doctor who has seen the deceased within fourteen days of the death. This goes to a third doctor, the Official Medical Referee, who also gives his permission. If there is any doubt at all about the circumstances of the death or the bona fide good wishes of the relatives, then the whole issue is referred to the Coroner who, if he is satisfied that all is in order, will issue his "Certificate E". If the Coroner is in any doubt about the immediate propriety of cremation, he may, of course, call for an inquest.

Immediately after the service, the coffin is removed to the vestibule and it, and its contents, cremated. There are usually four cremators in a crematorium, of which two are in operation at any one time. In any event, coffins and corpses are cremated within one hour of the end of the service. They are cremated singly: it could not be otherwise, for each cremator is capable of holding only one coffin. Cremators are usually gas fired, though there are some electrically fired; and new developments involve lasers. The cremator burns at between 800°C and 1200°C and the corpse and coffin are disposed of in one hour. Ash is collected in a large tray under the cremator and the bones ("calcium remains") still persisting are ground to a powder in a machine that resembles a spin-dryer.

Throughout the cremation proceedings, an identity card is kept by the coffin. Ashes are not confused, therefore. When relatives apply to recover the ashes, they can be certain they are those of the familiar deceased. Coffins are never opened in the crematorium, so stories about jewellery stolen are mostly unfounded. In fact, the staff are as decent and as reverent as anyone could hope to be in the circumstances.

The staff are not many: the Superintendent; two or three clerical staff; a chapel attendant who assists the Minister and the undertaker; someone in charge of flowers and music; one cremator operator; and a gardener. The cremator operator may hold a Certificate of Proficiency. Coffins are chipboard rather than oak or elm. There is an observation point at a tangent to the cremators from which relatives may observe the coffin enter the fire. This, I am informed, is not an option often taken up. It must be said that the whole thing is done as well as it might be.

Nonetheless, there are conspicuous ambiguities and cultural contradictions. The new god Science is worshipped at the cremator. There is computer control of the furnaces and an electronic readout of the goings-on. Whistles and bleeps are likely to sound if the temperature of the cremator falls below a certain figure, or if there is too much smoke or too much pressure. And yet, in the middle of all this hi-tech and scientific mastery, there seems to be a need for another sort of language altogether: as if in the ashes of scepticism and secularism, there must be some gesture towards a lost infinity. So the Application for Cremation form combines a thorough bureaucracy with a sham-antique religiosity or sentimentality. The declaration by the relatives is headed in gothic script:

The true answers to the questions set out below are as follows

At the same time, when it comes to paying for the cremation, the costs are set out in utilitarian typescript:

Fees for cremation (including Medical Referee & Burial of Ashes in Garden of Remembrance or Certificate of Cremation).

	£
Stillborn	–
Up to 1 year	–
Up to 16 years	–
Adult	87.00

Other fees

Ashes in Garden of Remembrance	7.50
Use of Chapel of Rest for 24 hrs	5.25
Cardboard Ash Box	1.75
Polytainer	2.10
Metal Urn	5.25
Oak Casket	15.00

Book of Remembrance

2 line entry	16.60
5 line entry	33.50
8 line entry	48.50

Memorial Cards

2 line card	8.50
5 line card	13.50
8 line card	19.00
Badges	19.00
Coat of Arms	29.50

(These prices include VAT at 15%)

Crocus bulbs per 100	6.50
Plaques including inscription (up to a maximum of 60 letters)	53.50
Plaque renewal fee for further 5 years	15.00

The most interesting of all the bureaucratic machinations is the nationally-agreed Code of Cremation Practice, for this shows up the unreconciled opposition of scientific-sceptical-cleanliness and outmoded-pseudo-religious-sentiment:

CODE OF CREMATION PRACTICE

1 CONDUCT
   The cremation of a human body is a highly emotional occasion for those taking part in the service. This must never be forgotten by the officials of the Crematorium, who must combine to create and maintain an atmosphere of reverence and respect throughout the entire proceedings.

2 STAFF

The greatest care must be taken in the appointment of members of the Crematorium staff, any one of whom may, by conduct or demeanour, detract from the atmosphere of reverence which it is endeavoured to create. When an appointment is made, preference should be given to certified applicants. In addition, it should be realized that the wrong type of man is capable of comment outside the Crematorium which can bring the Crematorium and Cremation into disrepute.

3 AFTER COMMITTAL

(a) A body shall not be removed from the Crematorium after the Service of Committal except for a lawful purpose.

(b) On the day when the Committal Service takes place, provided the necessary Authority to Cremate has been received, the coffin and its contents shall be put into the cremator exactly as they have been received on the catafalque and cremated.

(c) Once a coffin, with its contents, has been placed in the cremator, it shall not be touched or interfered with until the process of cremation is completed. On completion the whole of the Cremated Remains shall be collected and, following their reduction, shall be disposed of according to instructions received.

4 CORRECT IDENTITY

(a) No coffin shall be accepted at any crematorium unless it bears adequate particulars of the identity of the deceased person therein.

(b) Every care must be taken to ensure correct identification throughout the whole proceedings from the moment the coffin is received onto the catafalque until the final disposal of the Ashes.

5 SEPARATELY CREMATED

Each coffin given to the care of the Cremation Authority shall be cremated separately.

6 PRECIOUS METALS

Any precious metals found amongst the Cremated Remains, shall be disposed of in accordance with the directions of the Cremation Authority or higher Authority.

7 ASHES – CARE TO BE TAKEN

The utmost care shall be taken to ensure that the Ashes resulting from each cremation shall be kept separate. Following their removal from the cremator, the Ashes shall be reduced and placed in a separate container whilst awaiting final disposal. If the Ashes are to be strewn on the Garden of Remembrance, the ceremony shall be conducted with the greatest reverence and respect and in such a manner as not to leave the Ashes visible. When the Ashes are to be sent by rail or through the post, specially constructed containers shall be provided for this purpose, suitably labelled, and dealt with according to Recommendations laid down by the Federation of British Cremation Authorities in their special leaflet on this subject. Cremation Authorities shall ensure, by Regulation, that Ashes leaving their Crematorium always do so in a suitable type of container.

8 MECHANICAL APPARATUS

Cremators and all other mechanical apparatus used in the Crematorium shall be kept in good repair, and regularly overhauled and cleaned to ensure their being kept in perfect working order, and to prevent friction noises which will distract or disturb the mourners. Special attention shall be paid to mechanical devices which are particularly prone to develop imperfections. Every gas-fired cremator must be fitted with a solenoid valve safety device in order to reduce the possible risk of explosion when lighting up.

9 STATUTORY REGULATIONS

All cremations shall be carried out according to the provisions of the Cremation Acts 1902 and 1952 or any amendments thereof and the Regulations made thereunder, or under the appropriate statutory provisions and regulations applicable to the area in which a Crematorium is situate and, in those places where it is applicable, no cremation shall take place except on the written authority of the Medical Referee.

Just look at that first paragraph, "CONDUCT". There is a sort of bureaucratic attempt at religious sensitivity here. "The cremation of a human body is a highly emotional occasion . . ." Did we think it was not? They are trying to turn statements of the obvious into religious statements. The only sort of civilization or culture in which such a sleight of hand would even seem necessary is a secular and sceptical culture such as ours.

It is as if they feel guilty about the scientific-technological ambience and so they have to offer a few pseudo-religious excuses couched in language which is impersonal and archaic, a mixture of language, sort of bureaucratic-legal-masonic: ". . . of whom may by conduct or demeanour, detract from the atmosphere of reverence which it is endeavoured to create."

Note the deliberate air of seriousness. Those echoes, if not of the Prayer Book then at least of School Rules, in the phrase "conduct or demeanour". We do not try, but we "endeavour". We do not make, but "create". We are not far from the garden of Proserpine.

And then the office reasserts itself: "adequate particulars . . . provided the necessary authority" and so on. My remarks are not intended as any sort of judgement on the staff of the crematoria who, after all, are merely carrying out the wishes of society regarding its dead bodies. Rather, my observations are meant to make plain how our attitudes towards death, as towards everything else, have changed since our traditional way of living has given way to something else.

Whether you find what happens now cleaner, more civilized, more scientific and *therefore* better than what used to happen, is a matter of personal choice. But no personal choices can be made except under the authority of a culture and practice. It is a matter of opinion whether

59

our current rituals of disposal – abstracted, bureaucratic, impersonal and pseudo-scientific as they are – can truly bear the weight of our grief in the same way that more traditional practices did.

On the whole, I would prefer the front room, the piano and the failed aspidistra, the damp and the isolated clock – the sense that death is local, proximate and a present reality. "In the midst of life we are in death."

For, if we remove death from our immediate experience, we remove with it its palpable opposite: the zest for life itself.

Grief, Guilt and Bereavement

Bereavement is itself a kind of death. It provokes many of the same psychological moods and reactions as those which are discovered in the person who has been told that he will shortly die. The first and immediate reaction to the death of a near relative or friend is stark disbelief: how many times I have heard it said, "No, it's not true, it can't be! He hasn't gone."

Perhaps it is a sort of manic disbelief which even helps us cope in the moment of dereliction. As if, unconsciously, we imagine the deceased is still with us. Certainly it is true that all the great events of our human career are charged with energy that helps us cope with them. Birth, marriage and death – they are powerful religious-psychological moments. Jung called them "archetypal experiences". They are common in that they happen to us all, and uncommon in that they are unusual and so need to be coped with by ritual, common practice and traditional responses.

The funeral exists in order to help us cope with our grief. Often when I visit a bereaved person, he will say something like, "I mustn't show myself up in church." He means that he will try not to cry. But to help him cry, to give a rational human context to his distress, is what the funeral is for. Attempts to be euphemistic about death and disposal, though no doubt kindly-intentioned, actually undermine the bereaved person's capacity to grieve: and the expression of grief is absolutely necessary.

The words of the funeral service offer a final comfort in the hope of the resurrection of the dead. But there is no resurrection without a death. And the language used about death in the Book of Common Prayer is plain, stark – even bleak. It has its job to do. So, whatever other merits they may have, modern funeral services err psychologically when they remove all those words about "vile bodies", "worms destroy this body", "the bitter pains of eternal death" and so on. The modern services play up the joy of resurrection, but power drains away from this affirmation when the reality of death is glossed over. Death swallowed up, not so much in victory as in circumlocution. This is not a mere nicety of liturgical discussion but a vital issue in the psychological and spiritual care of the bereaved. As an emblem of what rites of disposal are about, we need no more than a look at their titles. The old book says, uncompromisingly, *The Burial of the Dead*. The new book is evasive: *Funeral Services* – a little too sanforized, like Consumer Services.

Let our hearts go out to the bereaved and let us do all we can for them, but let us not believe that we do anything at all for them by seeking, in any way, to minimize what has befallen them. Ashes to ashes, dust to dust . . . The burial in the churchyard is the archetypal symbol of death. How many novels, plays and films utilize this fact! For creative artists know that, for their work to carry conviction, it must portray reality, the truth. Bad art is a kind of lie. And so is euphemistic death. Human beings need to face up to what is and not what alternative looks cosier.

The crematorium has replaced burial in these days when all the churchyards are full. This need not be a bad thing, but in practice it is. The crematorium is a Municipal Euphemism – evasion on the rates. The thin, piped music which is just like the Muzak we hear everywhere else – except it might be in a minor key. The chromium and polished wheels on which the coffin is usually carried is redolent of the supermarket trolley: Consumer Services again. And the actual disposal – so vivid and visible in the churchyard – is removed from sound and sight. A curtain is discreetly drawn, as if death were nothing more than the happy ending of a night at the cinema.

It need not look like this. Many writers, appalled as I am by the present ignorance of what needs to be done in a funeral, have suggested rites and procedures in which the mourners could watch the coffin as it is taken into the furnace. But the mere suggestion of this possibility is enough to invite excoriation for copious inhumanity. It is not inhumane. Earlier, or other, civilizations with their funeral pyres knew what they were at. They were not less "civilized" than ourselves. They were certainly more religious. We are not helped in that backward glance towards the primitive terror by funereal Muzak, chromium and plush curtains.

When, as a society we become thus squeamish about death, then death gets the dominion over us. (It is a corroboration of much that Freud said to notice that the same thing has happened to sex.) When we do not, for whatever reason, cope with reality, then we lapse into neurosis. So our euphemized, tranquillized attitude towards death is neurotic. Death, and in particular the observation of other people's dying, has become . . . and I choose the word carefully, disembodied. TV and video death which children play at – just as they play at video rape in the playground. All is image and no reality. Zap! You're dead. A laser beam, a death ray. It is all rather like the violent cartoons in which the cat gets killed but invariably and painlessly – as in the Alternative Service Book's funeral rites – comes alive again.

In Huxley's *Brave New World*, where death has been officially euphemized by the State, children have classes which teach them (or rather condition them into) an acceptance of the event. The debate about sex education in our own country has been won by those who are in favour of it. I am in favour of death education – not as sponsored and provided by some Ministry of Thanatocracy – but by the making sure that our children take their places at the graveside and learn the reality of death. This cultural participation will help them cope with bereavement – and let it not be assumed that children avoid distress and the sense of loss which a death brings, by being excluded from the funeral because it is "not nice". Death is not nice. That is the brute reality before which all euphemisms and patterns of avoidance must evanesce. Perhaps it is even more important that children learn what death is, so that they will not come to regard it as what it is not: make-believe. Death sets a limit on human ambition, makes all but the most self-obsessed tyrant pause before action. If we constantly represent, in our video images, death as not so awful, then we cheapen our children's evaluation of the significance of life, of local, human lives as actually lived: with such consequences for violence and vandalism as are apparent already. Death teaches us that life is important, ultimately important because it is all we have. And this life which is ultimately important also, paradoxically for an ultimate thing, has its limits. Death is one of those limits. To begin to appreciate the value of life, then, is to know something of the reality of death. If this knowledge is withheld, out of a desire to protect the feelings of children, then they will as a result grow up neurotic about death and insensitive to life, because ignorant of its nature and value.

The funeral itself is not the only means of helping us cope with bereavement, and it is not the only aspect of death and grief to have become susceptible to euphemism. There are the ways of saying that someone has died, for instance: "passed away", "passed over" – and it is strange how nowadays the only use of "loved-one" means a dead loved-one. Euphemisms are attempts to subvert emotion. So it is no wonder that they generate a sort of heartlessness. I had visited an old lady in the hospital and then the hospice for months while she courageously fought a painful and demeaning last illness. We had many talks about pain, about life, death and religion. I had hoped to be with her at the moment of death, but it did not work out like that. When the hospice told me she had died, they said she had "passed away". Well, whatever had happened to her in the last throes of her life and in all our talks, it was not adequately judged in the phrase "passed away". I felt that all she had been through was thereby reduced. When Jesus came to the tomb of Lazarus, he had the grace to say plainly, "Lazarus is dead." The old lady would have liked the same to be said of her, I am sure.

The euphemism: it is invented in order to spare feelings when, precisely, feelings do not need to be spared but spent. If we are not allowed to feel horror-struck dereliction at the loss of a loved-one, what did we mean, even, by calling him a loved-one?

Another source of euphemistic insensitivity is in the medicalization of death. The wife of an old man in our village died. The GP, young, bursting with good intentions, came on the scene. He told the old boy, "Take two of these tablets. They're for mild anxiety." Now, I know there is a medical definition of "mild anxiety" – it exists in order to differentiate "severe anxiety". But, by using a technical phrase in (literally) a homely context, the well-meaning GP introduced an insensitive medicalization of the old man's distress. When your wife of fifty years – you could see him thinking – dies, you get mild anxiety, do you? What must happen before you get severe anxiety?

The death of a child, or a stillbirth, is thought to be especially upsetting, and so in this case even more strenuous attempts are generally made to prevent any association with what is actually going on. Commonly, when there is a stillbirth, the hospital authorities will volunteer to dispose of the corpse "unseen". A decent, dignified funeral is what the parents really need – and, it is important for the priest to tell them that they need it even if they do not want it. With the passage of time they will come to see that it was the right thing. Anything else – the anonymous shuffling-off of tragedy – will come to be seen as an evasion of reality that undermines the psychological and spiritual life of the grieving parents: makes of death a double deprivation.

A death in the close family leaves the survivors shocked and bewildered. This is so even if the dying has been gradual, not unexpected; even if the last illness has been so distressing that relatives prayed for the death of their loved-one as the only relief. This unavoidability of shock and bewilderment is because of the absolute, felt psychological difference between life and death. Even a very ill person is alive, has continuity, duration. Death is the opposite. Everything simply stops. This may seem a banal or even a meaningless thing to say, but it needs saying as the true description of psychological, emotional reality – a reality not generally understood until the irreversible event takes place.

The experience of the loved-one's death is radical and new. Whatever they imagined it was going to be like, they are nearly always shocked: "I hadn't bargained for this." Often, if the dying person has been nursed at home or visited regularly in hospital, the first reaction to the death is literally and physically one of loss: the bereaved no longer has anything to do; a constant responsibility has gone for ever. There is no cause even to go and fill up the water-glass any longer. I have heard people say, "I just didn't know what to do any more."

And then what dawns is that this new status quo really is irreversible. Things will never be the same again. Not only shall I not need to refill the water-glass this afternoon, but I shall *never* need to refill it. The havoc that death plays with our apprehension of time, activity and responsibility is . . . well, exactly, shattering. Someone has died. A world has been shattered. The task that even became a chore, I would now give anything to be able to do once again. There is thus a feeling of powerlessness and, not long delayed, a worse feeling of guilt: "I can't *even* refill the glass for her!"

When the suffering person dies, the suffering of the living begins. Because we can do no more to help them, we feel we ought to have done more while they were alive. This feeling is irrational, but that does not diminish its power over us. I have known people who nursed their dying wives or husbands day and night, months on end, taking little sleep, taking utterly no thought for themselves. Yet these are often the ones who suffer most after the death of their spouse. "I could have done more. If only I could have eased his mind. If only . . ."

And now all that is left for the bereaved is, "Tomorrow and tomorrow and tomorrow". Nursing a dying person is one of the most basically human and intimate of all actions, and so, exhausting and distressing as it must be, it also, rightly, confers on the nursing relative or friend a sense of value and significance. Something necessary is being done. Or rather, it is being done one minute and the next minute it is done no longer. The consequence is a sense of futility: "There's nothing I can do." And then, "I couldn't prevent his death." Guilt. "My caring was useless. He died anyway." The final stage of this self-denigration, loss of purpose and despair, comes when the bereaved person makes a general proposition of the meaninglessness of life out of his dismay. "My caring came to nothing. It doesn't matter now whether I cared or I didn't care. *Nothing* matters."

It is awful to see this irrational despair dragging on in bereaved people for months and years. The particular futility which she felt when she could not avert her husband's death, grows and corrupts itself into a sort of spiritual, psychological cancer: into the affirmation of general futility and meaninglessness; into inertia and bitterness; into an unconsolable misery of existence which is a living death.

This is the spectre of death in all his forms. Whether you are awaiting your own imminent death, or nursing a dying friend, or grieving over someone who has died, death is deathly: stultifying. It calls to account and mocks all life's claims to be meaningful. "What can matter *now*?" asks the widow. And so the generalized propositions of despair built up out of raw experience: "Nothing matters."

Of course it is irrational. It is just as irrational as the feeling of youth in Maytime that all is charged with glory and splendour. But it is no less real for its being irrational. All the really significant aspects of human nature are irrational, part unconscious, emotional and haunted. Is love rational? But we do not dismiss it because it is not. Rationality is useful, utilitarian – something that can be worked out on a computer or by the manuals of logical theory. We are not only rational. We are moved by the depths of joy and woe, love and death, fear and fantasy: "We are such stuff as dreams are made on."[1]

Such meaning as we have is not – contrary to what we might think, or like to think – rooted in abstract metaphysical propositions about life, the universe and everything. It is based in daily routine and mundane (i.e. worldly) habit. Take away our egg and bacon, our nightcap or morning "constitutional", and we are out of sorts. It is a much more radical disturbance of the habitual scene when one near to us dies.

The most disturbing disturbances are local. When someone in the household dies, there are often actual scene-changes. My grandfather's bed had been in the sitting-room for ten years. I had come to think of the sitting-room as like that. When he died, it was, of course, removed. You might say, the sitting-room reverted to normality: but it was not normal to me, nor to anyone else who had lived those years in our house. The new, "normal" arrangement of the room was a perpetual reminder that he had gone. And I was a boy of eleven with other preoccupations and a field full of pals: imagine what it is like for the widow, then, as she enters the room first thing in the morning and the bed – which betokens its occupant – is no longer there. And here the carpet is a darker shade, not bleached by the sunlight. And what is to be done with the tray and the invalid's drinking cup? The persistence of these things in the absence of the person they were there to serve shows them up as meaningless. It is only a short step from that practical definition to the general assertion that *everything* is meaningless.

The task done and the meaning gone. There is a deep and lasting silence. "It's so quiet these days," is a common expression of how it feels. The silence, however, is not peaceful: there is often a queer sort of expectation that "he" will come back, speak to her, reassure her in some way that nothing has changed, all is as it was, all is well. This expectation of ghosts may extend to an apprehension of them – voices and visions. It is not unusual. It is not madness, but just what might be expected. What else, after fifty years of sharing the same rooms?

And then she keeps his pipe and mug. He haunts them. They mean nothing to anyone else. There is a problem with clothes and shoes. If she throws them out, she recriminates with herself because this is a way of rejecting him. If she keeps them in the wardrobe, she feels vaguely silly or even macabre: what use are they there? "They'll always be there if ever he needs them" – grief can drive folk to such irrationalities. A compromise is to give the clothes and shoes to a worthy cause: they are not then being *just* thrown out; some good is coming out of her misfortune.

The funeral can be a big help. But it is not, in a sense, long-lasting. It is like first-aid, or perhaps even surgery. But now it is the bereaved person who needs the nursing. Between the death and the funeral – those unreal days – friends and neighbours are always remarkably helpful. Nothing is too much trouble. They will stay the night with her, do the shopping, wash clothes, clean, make pies for the funeral tea – in short, do all and more besides. The funeral is the chasm. Before it, friends and neighbours are falling over one another to be associated with the bereaved; after it, they will cross the street to avoid her.

They avoid her because they do not know what to say. They do not know how to refer to the deceased, and yet they feel they ought to refer to him. Also, because we are defined by our relationships – the people we live with and among say who we are – they do not know how to refer to or be with the bereaved person. She was Jack's wife all those years: now who is she?

The funeral is a festival, emotionally charged, so many people all talking to her about him and her. This is what the ritual is for – and beer and ham are no less parts of the ritual than "worms" and "ashes to ashes". The funeral plugs an emotional gap with more emotion: "It's as if he hasn't gone!" But he has. And when she returns to the empty house to look once more through the collection of black-bordered cards, it will be to know that he has gone, that she inhabits an empty, unfriendly silence, haunted by guilt, recriminations and bitterness.

The funeral is a great symbolic event. As such it must be archetypal, nostalgic. The dead man is remembered, and the remembrance, tied to ritual and evocative music, is deliberately poignant – calling to remembrance. The weight of his presence overhangs the place. This is disturbing, but it is also a comfort: for what was and is personally vivid, significant, to the widow is being made, dramatically, an issue of public involvement. The funeral, though, is life's last territorial demand. After the service and the ritual of tea, talk and ham, it is, as many bereaved people have told me, ". . . as if he'd never been, never walked the earth". The disjunction is terrifying.

Friends and neighbours do not know what to say, and that is why they avoid her in the street. They may think she is "getting over it" and that if they mention the deceased it will "upset her" – as if it would bring him back to her memory. The truth is, she thinks of nothing else. He is always in her mind and memory. Only now she feels not eased and comforted by the fact – as she did when he

71

was alive – but vaguely embarrassed, guilty, not knowing what to make of her thoughts. Should she try to forget? Perhaps that would take away the pain, but it would add to another sort of pain: guilt. "You've forgotten him!" Besides, if she does not think about him, what is there for her to think about? He was the centre and meaning of her life, a living landmark for so many years: she does not, cannot, know how or what to think now that he is no longer with her.

What, above all, she needs to be told, reassuringly, is that her life with him was indeed of infinite value; it was something which made her and him what they were together. She needs to talk about him, as, in the winter evenings, she needs to take out the old photographs and weep that mixture of joy and loss over them – without feeling ashamed. And so she needs neighbours and friends who are neither gauche nor squeamish, but who will come up to her in the street and ask her how she is, talk about the old times when her husband was still alive. I am not saying that it is easy for a neighbour to do this, but it is necessary work: she should not be left comfortless.

What about the relatives of the deceased? Should she see them? It all depends upon how they got on when he was alive. If there was a family feud, if she did not get on with her in-laws, then it may seem artificial to seek them out at this time. On the other hand, death can effect reconciliations, and, in any case, the funeral may have provided an opportunity for any icebreaking to be done. Death is an archetypal experience. It is charged with meaning and incomprehension, with inevitability and shocked outrage. In such a powerful atmosphere, sometimes the warring aspects combine to produce a strange rapprochement between people who have not spoken for years.

Or it may be that she has always got on very well with her late husband's parents. This often means (thankfully) that wife and in-laws can sustain and help each other now that he has gone. But it must always be remembered that, whatever he was to his mother and father, sister or brother, he was something quite different to his wife: each side will be jealous of their own image of who the deceased was. The need is for sensitivity. It is appalling when conversations between for example spouse and in-laws degenerate – as I have often seen them do – into friction and hatred:

> "He always said you never understood him. He never felt part of his family."
> "I could never tell what he saw in you in the first place; and I told him so, over and over again."

These conversations do happen. They are a sign of our unredeemedness. It is best if the privacy of these close relationships can be maintained after he has died in the same way that it was generally maintained while he was alive. Do not be jealous, anxious or annoyed because you could not be to him everything his mother was. You were not his mother, but his wife. And mothers-in-law, sisters-in-law and other close relatives must realize that they do not have copyright on the deceased. It is hard for them to accept that his wife understood (literally, "knew") him in a different way from them. The family bereavement offers ample choice for mutual help, deepening of one's knowledge not just of the deceased, but of one another. It can be a hell of jealous embarrassments. Or, with care and patience, it can be "A cup of strength to some poor soul, In his great agony." To wife and blood-relative alike.

A couple who have been married a long time look back upon the years of their marriage with affectionate nostalgia. There are the summer evenings of courtship. Christmas celebrations. The young children. While they are together, the long memory is a comfort and strength to them. When one partner dies, the memory remains for the other. And, instead of being a comfort, it can become a torment. A torment of grief and unrequitedness. A torment of guilt. For human beings persecute themselves with greater severity than any torturer. A simple guiltiness, such as may arise from the fact that she was not by his bed every second during his last illness can become compounded into an irretrievable sorrow over things done years, decades ago. Petty squabbles and rows of forty years back can assume a portentousness that can hardly be borne when he has gone.

And as memory fades, invention supervenes. So, if there is in reality nothing in the past with which she can reproach herself, she will make up some fault, flaw or cause of regret and so turn the happy remembrance of things past into torment.

Always, but especially in bereavement, we must learn a little gentleness with ourselves. No use eating ourselves as the moth frets the garment. So it is important for the bereaved person to get the memories on her side in the battle against loneliness and despair. There were happy times when he was alive. Let the happiness of those times be a help and consolation. The smiles on the old photographs were genuine enough. Grief and despair have a destructiveness about them: they can turn happy recollections into causes for sorrow and regret. It is important to fight with your whole humanity against this satanic destructiveness. Get the memories on your side. They were happy memories while he was alive. Nothing has happened since – what could possibly have happened? – to alter their substance. So let them now especially be a consolation.

Leaving aside neurotic guilt about the past, there may be moments of genuine regret over actual misdoings. What about the time when he . . . and I . . . when it really was my fault. I let him down . . . made him unhappy. There are ways of coping with this torment – a torment which is intensified by its very privacy: you are the only person in the world who now can recollect the original incident.

First, set the painful recollection in the context of many happy memories. Certainly it was real. It happened. But it was not the only thing that happened between you. And all the good things that you shared are more than enough to outweigh it. Secondly, and I know this is a desperate measure, call up the tormenting memory one more time. Let it have full rein. Go through the appalling incident with all its horror from start to finish. Then make some act of exorcism: literally and physically cast it out. We are still, at this late stage of the decline of our religious sensibilities, susceptible to ritual and the *gesture* or the sacramental act. It may be a time for burning a photograph or an article of clothing, a letter. Do it then. And, at the same time, if you still believe you were in the wrong, own up to the wrong – aloud if need be, if possible, with "wailing and gnashing of teeth".

Then forget it.

Cast it into the darkness of the grave. Let it be buried with all that does not deserve recollection, all that destroys and dissipates fond remembrance. Remember the sunlight and his eyes when they were full of tenderness. And you were together. You *were* together. Your love was real. And there is nothing to regret, nothing for which now, in your loneliness, you should persecute yourself. Dark memories are satanic, and they need to be exorcized. Happily you have within you the power to work the exorcism – without benefit of clergy.

It is not the memories themselves which have changed, but their context. Once they were a part of a shared life; now they are shades of desolation. The other person on the photograph is no longer there. All the talk about the past which belonged to "us" is now only set in the lonely concept, "me". Many widows stil use "we" in the context of the present tense, so deep is the affiliation with the deceased.

There is another sort of guilt. If she finds any joy or comfort with someone else, she feels it is an insult to his memory, an undervaluing of what they had together. The most difficult aspect of this is new, shared intimacies. The dead husband (and let us not forget the same applies to a wife) did things this way: making tea or making love – patterns of intimacy persist and alterations to the pattern cause confusion and mixed feelings. One whole half of bereavement *is* guilt. She finds a new friend. Perhaps he is lonely too. There is some mutual gratification. But now she says to herself, "I didn't do so-and-so for him while he was alive; now I'm making things worse by what I'm doing after he's gone."

Guilt the great stultifier. It jaundices feeling and paralyses action. Bereaved people must learn to have some sympathy with themselves. What has happened to them is terrifying. This awful event should not be emotionally reinforced so that the sufferer feels imprisoned in guilt and loss. She has needs. They are *needs*, not indulgences. She must be as kind to herself as she would, at her best, like to see herself being to her husband's memory.

Almost anything that anyone says, even in sympathy, can be turned into pain. "Life must go on," is a familiar saying. But life as she knew it for perhaps half a century

76

is not going on – because he is not going on. The map has been amended and all the landmarks changed. A frequent expression of bereavement, "He was always *there*". This is what is meant by context, emotional and personal, familar context. And, in a sense, he is still there: the constant self-judgement is two-way: she feels guilty about things she did not do for him – or the bad way she treated him – while he was alive; now that he is dead the memory of him is a judgement on all she does. "It is", as one woman said to me, "as if he's looking over my shoulder, watching my every move."

This is what is meant by a haunting. Not a silly, scary-film business, but a sense that all your present activities are observed and judged by someone who, being dead, has acquired a sort of ultimate authority. Each man's death diminishes me: precisely. I am not free to be myself in the haunting presence of the intimate dead. Is it possible to turn what were once happy, shared memories, but which then became sad, difficult and lonely ones, back into something encouraging again?

One great difficulty that stands in the way is simply that people – friends, relatives, neighbours – do not understand what the bereaved person is going through. The experience of being bereaved is not something you can know until it happens to you. And yet all feel they know how to sympathize. They do not. They do not, generally, perceive the anxiety that they cause when they urge you to "snap out of it". This is because they see you as a single person again. And this you are not: you are a lonely person with an ineradicable personal memory of shared intimacy. You are followed around by a shadow. Anything said to you is, as it were, also said to the deceased.

It is as well to say at the start that there is not always

a cure for every form of human unhappiness. It is also as well, though painful, to be reminded that, with a death, certain things have come to an end: an individual life and, for the wife or husband, a shared life. It is possible to survive even this dereliction – "survive", I think, being the word rather than any victorious phrase such as "triumph over". The hurt will always be there, as memory and guilt cast their twin shadows.

But the ability to cope when he has died, does not begin with or at the moment of bereavement: it is something for which the whole of your previous life has been a preparation. It is banal, but true, to say that all we have is our experience and what we have made of it. We are ourselves as we ourselves have created ourselves.

One of the most important duties in life – all your life – is to take note, not to let things pass us by, not to be inadvertent. If we do not notice things, then we shall not be armed with the wonder of them against the ill that befalls us. All the great hymns of praise and giving glory to God are not for His benefit. He does not need anything. They are to direct our minds and hearts to what is glorious in the world, so that we shall not give up hope, not – as the gospels say – "be left comfortless". The other great importance is not to take anything for granted. That is what is meant by all the scriptural passages about the judgement coming "as a thief in the night" and "This night thy soul is required of thee." As the Prayer Book says, "In the midst of life we are in death." It is well to have a realistic though not a morbid recollection of this truth.

So, if we notice the world and the glory of it and if we do not take it for granted – which after all is only another way of saying the same thing – then we shall have, as consequence, something approaching a vocational attitude towards life. This is regarding ourselves as belonging, recognizing our individual importance, but acknowledging that there is something – a task, an awed and reverential demeanour before the order and mystery of creation – which is greater than ourselves. The institution of marriage, for instance. So we may come to see it not just as a social policy or convention, or as a means of distributing domiciliar and sexual privileges, but as something to which we are called. And, as we are called, so we are defined. The institution of marriage, for all the time that we are married, describes and prescribes whom we are. "Till death us do part", is not a piece of callousness – as if the Prayer Book cares nothing for our distress. It is at once the announcement that one vocation has ended, and another has begun. Can we learn to live bereavement, and whatever goes with it, as a new calling? "Life goes on." Better it be something to which we feel truly called, and therefore to which we can truly belong – because, it, the new experience, also describes who we are.

> What we call the beginning is often the end,
> And to make an end is to make beginning.
> The end is where we start from.[2]

But the poet does not mean to suggest that ends and beginnings are easily separated. However new the beginning after the loss of a marriage partner, much of the life that was lived before the end and beginning of bereavement will remain. It will always be impossible for her to think of certain places, food, music, etc. without calling him to mind. Nor is it desirable that she should try to forget, to sever these links. The vocation of bereavement is to carry those memories and associations into the new life and to let them be forces for constructiveness, not destructiveness.

It is hard to achieve this and painful. But the refusal to try leads only to the misery of bitterness and self-pity. An acceptance of the memories is painful, but at least it is constructive, restorative pain. "Do this in remembrance of me," has psychological and spiritual connotations which extend beyond the service of Holy Communion. Memory can be a celebration, sacramental, redemptive. When Jesus said those words to his disciples, he did not mean, "Remember me and be miserable." Quite the opposite. It is possible to make all our remembrances redemptive. Can she begin by trying to be thankful for the time they had together? When that tearful rush of a seaside recollection, a happy holiday, overtakes her, can she learn, in the agony of her loss, to be warmed by gratitude for the cause of the recollection – the happy holiday itself? She might even want to say aloud something like, "Well, didn't we have a marvellous time in Scotland, Jim!"

Talking thankfully to children and grandchildren about the past helps too. Shared happy recollections are doubly powerful. But it is usually best to banish any unhappy ones from family conversation. The old saying, "One should only speak good things of the dead", is a wise one. First, for the very good reason that the dead cannot answer back, answer any accusations. Secondly, because while shared happy memories are restorative, the communal harping on bad times perpetuates the misery of them. When a bad or a sour memory arises, look it in the face and cast it out. Cast it out by remembering the good.

Most important of all, it should be remembered that there is not complete triumph over the pain and sorrow of bereavement: no "counselling" . . . "expert" . . .

"technique" . . . for altogether doing away with woe. What would it mean if there was such a technique? It would undervalue the shared relationship which has now ended. It would reduce human life, in the person of the bereaved, to something like automation – life lived as a conditioned reflex. The worst thing is not feeling anything. That is far worse than the pain. We are never entirely free from pain at any stage in our lives. That does not matter. What does matter, what determines the sort of people we are becoming as we grow and age, is how we adjust to the pain, what we do with it. Growing and ageing: a word for the aim of these processes is "maturity".

If each man's death diminishes me, it is also true that each man's death helps me. For there is a solidarity in bereavement, as in life. The bereaved person knows that others have suffered this same loss before him: sometimes the exchanged glances at the old folks' meetings are poignant, full of a sad but shared recognition. In shared suffering we find our common humanity. So, while the bereaved person needs solitude, it is helpful too if he spends some of his time with others who are in the same plight.

* * *

Of all bereavement the loss of a child is most agonizing. It is possible to be reconciled to the death of an adult: all life does come to an end. But added to the feeling of loss at a child's death, is the sense that life is purposeless or, worse, malign. The question, "Why?" is here most unanswerable. The most desolate funerals are those of children. Once – it seemed cruel coming so soon after the joyful alleluiahs of Easter – I stood on the chancel step, gazing down the whole length of the nave to the open west door and the cherry blossom beyond. The undertaker came in carrying the tiny coffin in front of him. There were only the two of us. We stood facing each other over the absurd coffin. We said very little, but what depths of human feeling called out to each other. In a way, this also showed the triumph of humanity even over meaningless-ness and despair: for we had solidarity even, especially, in this.

The parents could not bring themselves to attend the church ceremony, and so they waited up at the crematorium for us to be done with the main part of the service; all they wanted to hear were the words of committal. I was glad that they could bring themselves to do that much at least, for the finality of death must be acknowledged or else the pain is worse. Even purposelessness needs to be clothed in a ritual gesture if we are to abide it.

There are no abstract theological justifications of death, and particularly the death of an infant, which do any good at all. Everything falls by the side of the brute fact: "Rachel weeping for her children and will not be comforted for they are not." No words about heaven and the life everlasting will help. They want to know, rightly, why they were allowed to labour at the pregnancy and birth, to prepare fully, to go through the creative trauma of delivery, only to lose the whole aim and object of their expectation. There is no reply. All answers and explanations are more or less glib. So, life is purposeless then, or else malign? Not at all.

Purpose and meaning and goodness and love are all there in the human sympathy and affection of those who arrange and attend the obsequies. There are friends and relations, of course. But the ordinary human concern of the undertaker, the sexton, the parson and the passers-by who behold these things from afar, shows that humanity, so wounded, bands together even in despair. You want to know where purpose and meaning are in such an event? Where has goodness gone? Look into the faces of those who stand in the rain at the cemetery. It may be that God is in his heaven and all is right with the world, but it is foolish, useless and wicked to make that assertion at the death of a child. It may be that God is infinitely merciful, and that he will wipe away all tears from our eyes. But, at the moment, it is the aunt or uncle, the sister or wife who holds your hand while you are crying. "No one", said George Eliot, "ever heard the divine pity except by lips that were moved by human pity." That is the consoling, purposeful human truth beyond all the pseudo-religious excuses and metaphysical hot air.

We were never promised that we would not be broken, really broken; but that we shall be put together again. After death the resurrection. Else there were no resurrection. Bereavement is the form death takes in life. Comfort and human pity are the earthly manifestations of resurrection. The funeral is the end and the beginning. It disposes of mortal remains and it is meant to begin our deliverance from grief.

That is why it is crucial. In the case of the death of a very young child or an infant, it is common for sincerely motivated professionals to discourage elaborate ritual, "a fuss" as it is sometimes said. A couple in my parish suffered the coming of their first child, stillborn. It happened at one o'clock in the morning. The father left his wife's hospital bedside when, at seven o'clock, she had finally fallen asleep. He asked the Ward Sister how he might go about receiving the body of his son and making arrangements for the funeral. "You'll have to wait until the Administration Block opens at nine-thirty." (Administration Block – what accidental poignancy our language holds!)

The Administrator told him not to worry, to go back to his wife and they, the Authorities, would supervise the disposal. A few days later he would be able to collect the ashes and have a short ceremony at the corner of the municipal cemetery. It was all so kindly meant – to try to preserve the parents against *unnecessary* grief. But grief is necessary. The young man knew this, and so he persisted. The Administrator was dedicated to his system and not easily moved. His last discouragement – the most potent of all in a materialistic society – was, "It'll cost you money, you know!"

The young man paid, and we buried little David after a short service in the village church. Now they have two thriving children, but their father told me: "I needed David's funeral. I needed it. There was nothing else I could do." How frequently our attempted kindness kills. Out of pure kindness misplaced, that Administrator would have denied the man the only thing that could help him: the ritual acceptance of an inescapable tragedy.

Thankfully, there are paradoxical graces. The death of a child is a more acute pain than the death of an adult, but it is less of a chronic ache. This is because the very sharpness of the tragedy – the brevity of the child's life – limits the memory of him. Perhaps he never grew old enough to speak? As time passes, his existence is remembered not as a chronicle of exchanged emotions, but as a simple event. When the emotional memories have not had the opportunity to become attached, the event fades.

At the death of a child, the parents' worst feeling, once

the funeral is over, is guilt. "We let him down." It is the maternal instinct thwarted. They feel that they could not do *anything* for him. It helps if they can have another child. Not as any sort of "replacement" but as a confirmation of their worth. They feel they have failed. The new child constitutes at least a partial success. The darkness within us will use any means to foster our self-hate. The death of a child is an ideal opportunity for the lurking Shadow to twist the screw of our masochism. We must learn a little gentleness with ourselves, learn to banish the self-hate and love ourselves a little – so that we may love our neighbours as ourselves.

Is the death of a teenage child the worst of all? Here there has been the chance for a relationship to form and for memories to accrue. The teenage death seems also even more pointless than the death of a child. "If God knew he was going to take her at fifteen, why didn't he take her at birth, and have done with it?" Such outbursts show the feelings of anger against an apparently senseless waste of life.

Yet the way in which some young people show courage in the face of death is moving and helpful. I knew a girl, Alison, who had suffered from kidney disease all her life. Constantly in and out of hospital. Dialysis with all its indignities and limitations. In years I never heard her complain. When she was seventeen, she received a kidney transplant and she and her parents were filled with hope. But their hope was not fulfilled and Alison declined. She knew she was dying and she set about the task with selflessness and serenity. As she lay in the hospital she had a sort of innocent maturity about her. Not at all sentimental, mock-religious. She was genuinely more interested in how I was getting on, about the parish and the village, than about her own case. Lives and deaths like

Alison's are not pointless, because they are examples to us. To say her death was meaningless is as if we were to say that Christ's death was meaningless. All suffering, and particularly that bravely borne, is redemptive.

Alison learned to die as we all must learn to die, and she did it well. So we must all learn to cope with bereavement. That "must" has no cold theological or moral force about it – stiff upper lip, duty to God and doing the right thing. It is simply that, face to face with the inevitabilities, we may as well find the right way to cope with them than the hundreds of wrong ways. It is like learning to bend and pick something up from the ground, or like playing a stroke at cricket: the right way looks right, feels right and turns out to be the most economical and efficient way of performing the act. To grieve well and to suffer loss nobly, learning from the experience, growing more mature and whole by it, assuages the grief and helps compensate for the irretrievable loss itself.

We become mature, whole, by changing those things which need changing but also by adjusting ourselves to what is inevitable. As I said at the start of this chapter, so much in contemporary society seems to try to convince us that there is no death, no loss and bereavement. Euphemisms. The Administration Block. Piped Muzak at the crematorium. All these things are, however kindly-intentioned, utimately against us: for they all teach us that things are other than they are. But to live as if it were other than it is, is to fall into neurosis. Unfortunately, neurotics too still have to live: only they have neurotic pains and subterfuges added to the natural suffering which all life entails. In the end the easiest way is the right way, the way which accepts the unavoidable woe as well as the surprising joys. It cannot be wrong to live in reality and to eschew delusion.

The comforts I have been trying to point to: Forgive the wrongs and hurts in the memories. Do not forget him. Call him to mind often. Talk about him. Talk *to* him. Be assured that others have felt what you now feel. And, in consequence, feel a solidarity with them. Remember, it is not wrong or weak to weep. It is inevitable that you feel some guilt. We all do. Be a little gentler with yourself. Let the examples of others inspire and comfort you. There is nothing wrong with depending on people: people are all we have.

Religion – not in the preaching, "ramming it down your throat" sense – is a help. In the broadest sense. The words, music and icons of the Christian faith are the property of us all in Europe. I look, in my loss, at Velasquez's *Crucifixion* – and there are dozens of depictions of this terrible event by other artists – and I see a portrait of pain and horror, but also of acceptance, love and tenderness. Here is the man of sorrows and acquainted with grief. Even if the whole Christian story was made up, and patent invention – though I do not believe it was – great art does not tell lies.

Whatever you feel in your sorrows, the man in that picture feels it too. But look at the infinite tenderness!

> Did ere such love and sorrow meet
> Or thorns compose so rich a crown?[3]

Suicide

In Christian society, suicide is a sin and, as used to be the rule, the body of the suicide is buried in unconsecrated ground. This is because suicide is an act of desperation which implies a lack of belief in the Almighty and purposeful God, creator of heaven and earth, origin of man's being. As an act, suicide is the sacrament of despair. Perhaps it is close to, or even to be identified with the unforgiveable sin – blasphemy against the Holy Spirit – because it calls into question the goodness of God. If there is a God, there is no need for us to despair, for he will finally redeem us from whatever woes we endure here. The Church teaches that there most certainly is a God. Thus to despair of God's mercy, even to doubt his existence, is a sin. In the old and, in this case, ironic language, a "mortal" sin. And a sin that cannot be repented.

This account of things was believed when Christianity was at its most influential, in the Middle Ages. In those days, the Christian faith was not just an aspect of life, among other things; it was an explanation of all life, and, more than an explanation, a way of being in the world. It enclosed all art and science, and theology was the Queen of Sciences.

A man might kill himself in the Middle Ages, for the same reasons as some kill themselves today – because he was poor or intolerably unhappy. But he knew what sort of act he was thereby committing. The rash act. The blasphemous act.

Then came science in its modern sense of enquiry unblinkered by dogma, and philosophy not as the handmaid of theology but as a free, speculative technique. The being and goodness of God was called into question. The medieval religious world-picture was no longer taken for granted as simply the way things are.

This was the occasion of cultural fragmentation. In politics, the nation-state supplanted the homogeneity of the Holy Roman Empire. Luther against the Pope. In the individual it divided soul from body. The medieval system was a whole, literally an incarnation of sensible particulars. There was no split between mind and body, no discontinuity between this world and the next. It was a wonderful order of angels and men with God at the summit: and this was mirrored in the social life of feudalism, with the King as the divine representative.

All this collapsed at the Renaissance. In painting, men and women and landscapes were the subject-matter, and not the religious images of earlier times. Rising science looked at the universe not as a mystery to be apprehended in awe and wonder, but as a puzzle to be solved. Man appointed himself measure of all things.

The split in consciousness was demonstrated superbly in two classic texts of European literature: Descartes's *Meditations* and *Hamlet* by William Shakespeare. Descartes began in abject uncertainty, questioning everything. In Bertrand Russell's words, "Is there any knowledge in the world so certain that no reasonable man could doubt it?" The question would not have occurred to the medieval mentality, when it was believed that there was such a thing as dogma, or revealed truth. Descartes cast everything into doubt. His programme of Systematic Doubt led him to the conclusion that the only thing of which he could be certain was that he doubted.[1] I doubt, therefore I think; because I think, therefore I am. *Cogito ergo sum*.

It would not have occurred to a medieval philosopher to think that mere thought was what guaranteed being. Consider the lilies of the field . . . True, Descartes went on to deduce, first the existence of God from this *Cogito*, and then to marshal arguments to prove the existence of the external world (and of the human body). It would not have seemed other than insane to the medieval philosopher to have to *demonstrate* in argument that the world "out there" exists.

Descartes did not say, "I farm, therefore I am." His definition of man is that of the disembodied thinker. As far away from the medieval incarnational outlook as you can get. For example, it is instructive to notice that the cathedrals of the Middle Ages were not signs and symbols – "images" of heaven and eternity – but actual embodiments of it. The doctrine of transubstantiation was not invented in order to demonstrate the otherworldliness of Christ, but his reality as bound up with the sorrows of this world.

Descartes and Shakespeare were still writing in the early interim. They did not have the full confidence of modern atheistic science which has, as Laplace said, "No need of the God-hypothesis". We must, in our enlightenment, excuse their reticence, and bear with them while they are yet unwilling entirely to cast away a thousand years of traditional believing.

Their writings still lean towards the world whose creator and King is God, the Father of our Lord Jesus Christ. But they are worried. They are caught mid-epoch. Each writes the work of true tragedy because each writes with a faith undermined and with a modernity unconsolidated. It is almost as if in this "brave new world", a place must be found for God who has recently become superfluous to philosophical requirement.

Descartes is not really interested in God, or even in proving God's existence. What he is really about is proving man – proving that man has the capacity truly to know things. And one of the things man can know – almost by chance – is God. Shakespeare's *Hamlet* takes things a stage further and reflects the profound unease which the collapse of medieval certainties has generated in Renaissance man. The play is superb because it is a play of crisis, a tragedy. As Hamlet is locked in indecision, vacillating, so is Shakespeare, caught between the medieval world and the new scientific age emerging. He cannot, for all his lucid scepticism, free himself from the constraints of the earlier world-view. His language is therefore creative and conservative. Its subject is suicide:

> To be or not to be: that is the question:
> Whether 'tis nobler in the mind to suffer
> The slings and arrows of outrageous fortune,
> Or to take arms against a sea of troubles,
> And by opposing end them?[2]

Suicide is that deliverance, that "quietus" which can be made "with a bare bodkin". This is modern, scientific. The man is seen as co-terminous with his corporeality: he dies with the death of his body "and there's an end on't". It is also ethically modern in that Shakespeare ignores the blasphemous nature of the rash act. Man may his own quietus make, and what has this to do with God and the faded medieval splendour?

The question is about being, the nature of being. And the answer, in Shakespeare and Descartes, is very similar: "I *think* therefore I am" and "whether 'tis nobler in the *mind*". The true spirit of the Renaissance – the mind of man as the measure of the world.

But there is a hangover. Shakespeare goes on:

> To die: to sleep;
> No more; and by a sleep to say we end
> The heartache and the thousand natural shocks
> That flesh is heir to, 'tis a consummation
> Devoutly to be wished.[3]

There is the mind of the Renaissance scientist, inferring that all flesh is grass, material; and so death is a passing into sleep – that is all. But then:

> To die, to sleep;
> To sleep: perchance to dream: ay, there's the rub.
> For in that sleep of death what dreams may come
> When we have shuffled off this mortal coil,
> Must give us pause.[4]

Shakespeare cannot escape entirely from the medieval picture. The dreams of heaven and hell, are they real? And the materialist doctrine is discarded in the phrase, "shuffled off this mortal coil". For, what has done the shuffling-off? Why, the soul. It can mean nothing else. It is not hard to imagine what was at the back of Shakespeare's mind – the Bible and:

> Fear most unnatural, yet now
> The shadows creep on, we know not how.[5]

Descartes's predicament was the same only it was expressed academically rather than personally and dramatically: what is the point of linkage between mind and matter, the unextended and the extended? The Middle Ages had an answer: Incarnation. And there it was in doctrine and stone. Shakespeare and Descartes had only inspired disjunction, disunity. And Geulinx's attempt to reconcile the Cartesian dualities by recourse to an analogy about mind and matter governed by two distinct but exactly synchronized clocks is too far-fetched even for scholastic philosophy.

Since the Renaissance we have not known what manner of men we are. Are we body? Or mind? Or some curious interaction? So, because we cannot solve this problem, we live the life of confident materialism haunted by divine and devilish fantasies. Only, the Renaissance changes the act of suicide from one that is explicitly a denial, blasphemous, into something like an experiment – precisely, a scientific experiment. Hamlet's soliloquy in Act III has the air of conjecture and hypothesis about it. What will happen if I do this?

Moreover, Shakespeare knows that hypotheses are not reality. He speaks of resolution "sicklied o'er with the pale cast of thought". And he has a medieval cosnciousness of sin – something which does not sit easily with the brave new world of science, material causation and scepticism with regard to all things spiritual:

> The fair Ophelia! Nymph, in thy orisons
> Be all my sins remembered.[6]

But what induces the suicidal disposition in Hamlet? He has, of course, what we should refer to as his "Personal Difficulties" – "the incestuous bed", the ghost of his father and so on. But are these not problems he can solve? He could kill the man who has usurped his father's throne and dishonoured his mother. But he hesitates. And this is because the political, familiar problem is not the true problem. What the real trouble is, Shakespeare explains directly:

I have of late – but wherefore I know not – lost all my mirth, forgone all custom of exercises; and indeed it goes so heavily with my disposition that this goodly frame, the earth, seems to me a sterile promontory; this most excellent canopy, the air, look you, this brave o'erhanging firmament, this majestical roof fretted with golden fire, why, it appears no other thing to me but a foul and pestilent congregation of vapours! What a piece of work is a man! How noble in reason! How infinite in faculty! In form, in moving, how express and admirable! In action how like an angel! In apprehension how like a god! The beauty of the world! The paragon of animals! And yet, to me, what is this quintessence of dust?[7]

This is the expression of a man who has lost his faith, his sustaining world-view. It is exactly what was happening all over Europe at the Renaissance. And, with the overthrow of a metaphysical world-view, comes the overthrow of ethics and all value:

There is nothing either good or bad, but thinking makes it so.[8]

Thinking again. Locked in the Cartesian mindblock. Unincarnated.

Luther is a stopgap, a sort of compromise. He tries to reinstate God and accommodate him to the new sense of isolated individualism. For Luther will not allow medieval Catholicism, the wonderful system of angels and men, with all the trappings of social-supernaturalism. Luther believes in "Me and My God". The individual can approach God on his own account, without recourse to the priests and their craft. This leads inevitably to a collapse of order and a decline into scepticism and relativism: if I may not make appeal to a church universal to tell me who God is, then how can I tell that the man who is standing next to me in the Reformation chapel believes, as he prays, in the same God as the God I believe in?

Protestantism and Reformation, a stopgap. An intermediate stage between the full-blooded Catholicism and incarnated view of the Middle Ages and, on the one hand, the out and out scepticism of Hume, Voltaire and Les Philosophes; and, on the other, the despairing religious-language-without-a-God of Schopenhauer, Kierkegaard, Nietzsche and the existentialists of the early twentieth century.

The failure of the medieval synthesis, incarnation, led to a loss of nerve and a loss of faith. Moreover, this was (and is) a loss which the new scientific world has not been able completely to assuage. We do not really believe that science can answer our deepest needs: we insist – though we may be embarrassed by the language – that our deepest needs are spiritual. The Romantic poets and the proto-existentialists of the eighteenth and nineteenth centuries despised science, saw its explanations as a caricature of human existence: so William Blake said of the greatest scientist:

> ... May God us keep
> From single vision and Newton's sleep.

And:

> Mock on, mock on, Voltaire, Rousseau;
> Mock on, mock on, 'tis all in vain!
> You throw the sand against the wind,
> And the wind blows it back again.[9]

George Eliot, asked by Comte to write a Socialist Utopia, said she could not "lapse from the picture to the diagram".

Coleridge said it in, "That willing suspension of disbelief for the moment, which constitutes poetic faith."

Kierkegaard went so far into explicit denial of the scientific era as to call one of his latest and finest works, *Concluding Unscientific Postcript*.

Our own century has observed again and again the tendency of scientific/technological-political utopias to turn into dystopias. There is Huxley's *Brave New World* with its "humans" who are only emancipated while their wills are circumscribed and their desires predicted. There is Orwell and his definition of scientific-material-socialism as a world of corrupt pigs. The prophets abound: Dickens railing against Coketown and statistics; Lawrence against the mentalizing of emotion; Leavis against "Technologico-Benthamism"; and T. S. Eliot spearing scientific culture as express sociology, men

> . . . dreaming of systems so perfect that no one will need to be good.[10]

There is the price of irony to pay. For these Romantic poets, prophetic iconolasts of science's citadel, could not themselves entirely return to the medieval synthesis; partly, of course, because it was primarily a political reality, and, as such, it had ceased to exist. No going back to no-man's-land.

So, denied the comforts of religion by the sceptical mind and refusing to give homage to the crassness and sheer spiritual vacuity of scientific-technological thought, how are we to live at ease? Not, how are we to live an easy life? Life was certainly not easy in the Middle Ages. But then that age had an incarnated view which held life and death together: two aspects of the one vibrant reality. Well, look at the cathedrals: nothing like them in Europe before or since. Were the Egyptians "primitive" for having built the pyramids? And what has modern science built? The H-bomb? Certainly. And the means of its deployment.

Of course, scientific-technological society can prolong life. This is sometimes regarded as something to be desired. But what the medieval theologian asked, what Shakespeare asked, what even such reprobates as Blake and Dostoevsky asked is, "What is life for?" Mere duration is not enough – especially, ironically, since Einstein has taught us lessons about the relative nature of time – and so we need not only width but quality; we ache to learn about values. Miracle vaccines free us from diseases which would formerly have killed. "Yes," said Dostoevsky, "Free from what . . . but free *for* what?"

The Renaissance divided art and science and – against the example of the medieval cathedral – put theology and technology in separate camps. Cosmology was no longer a theological-moral art as it had been in Dante. The telescope and the laws of planetary motion turned it into something merely mechanical – highly sophisticated, mathematically clever, but mechanical just the same.

This divide, felt so sharply by Shakespeare and Descartes, created a schism in European consciousness and produced in the drama men like Hamlet: intelligent men paralysed by doubt – the same doubt which Descartes formalized into a philosphical principle and which burgeoning science accepted as its method. Doubt; postulate; observe; experiment; conclude; affirm/deny.

In psychological-spiritual terms, this split showed itself as anxiety and neurosis. The old question about the meaning of life was no longer answered by a religious culture and civilization with its cycle of feasts and fasts, its dogmas incarnated in glass and stone, in processions and statues, in bread and wine at the altar. So where were people to look for meaning, for an answer to the problem of existence? Increasingly to the national religions – that direct historical/theological line which leads from Luther to Hitler, from Cromwell to the systems of Socialism and Communism. As science succeeded, religion became more and more marginalized and therefore more strident in the need to assert itself against the spirit of the age. So we finally see churches often behaving as publicity-conscious sects for the committed and the likeminded. Such organizations do not provide answers to the problem of meaning for more than a small minority of people.

Or else people turned to science and expected it to give answers which had formerly been given only by religion. In the nineteenth century, men like Comte, Feuerbach and Marx predicted that the scientific outlook, fuelled by industry, would be the new culture and civilization. And the old religious questions would not arise. Social Darwinians like Herbert Spencer believed that, as man had physically evolved from the apes, so his spiritual and moral evolution would be assured. Bentham, Mill and the Utilitarians looked forward to the day when social and moral difficulties would be solved by rationality and good will: Arnold's "sweetness and light".

But the religious questions have stubbornly refused to go away. We remain in the mind-split of Hamlet. Perhaps the world has no meaning? In a world without meaning, why not kill ourselves? Because, "To sleep, perchance to dream: ay, there's the rub."

Because we are afraid, and our very scepticism – not thinking itself capable of pronouncing on the nature of the afterlife (if any) – compounds our fear. As David Hume said, "We are not bribed to our existence by its delights, but we cling to it because of the terrors of the unknown."

Dostoevsky argues that suicide is a justifiable step on the grounds that life is a "comedy perpetuated by nature altogether stupid and I deem it humiliating for me to deign to play it. I condemn that nature which, with such impudent nerve, brought me into being in order to suffer."[11] So suicide is conceived as an act of revenge on an indifferent, "stupid" world.

However, while this argument may have a certain logical appeal, it goes against our instincts – not just the so-called "instinct to survive" but our commonsense and self-regard: it does seem, after all, an extreme way to venge oneself upon life by the method of self-extermination.

In *The Possessed* Dostoevsky gives us the character Kirilov who wants to kill himself because "it is *his* idea". It is an act of rebellion. He will assert his freedom by taking his own life. Nietzsche has a similar view of suicide, which he regards as the ultimate sign of freedom, a personally usable logical stop-card which is reserved for the direst emergency:

> The thought of suicide is a great consolation:
> by means of it one gets successfully through
> many a bad night.[12]

These suggestions by Dostoevsky and Nietzsche are not meant simply as answers to the problems of personal suffering, such as may arise out of poverty or an unhappy love affair. They are revolutionary answers to the problem of what life means – the problem unanswerable since the decline of medieval civilization. And this answer to the problem of meaning is that man himself, an individual, creates his own meaning. The truth of this proposition is, as it were, guaranteed by the fact that, on any bright May day when there is not even a cloud in the sky, a man can take a pistol and shoot himself in the head. Thus suicide becomes an escape from meaninglessness, from the "comedy" of life's sufferings endured without our asking; and also a way of affirming meaning as the ultimate expression of individual freedom. Logic may commend it, but most of us recoil from it.

Is there a way of reconciling ourselves to suicide, so that we do not regard it as a fearful and terrible act, but as something quite natural of which we shoud be unafraid?

Schopenhauer says, "In my opinion it ought rather to be demanded of the clergy that they tell us by what authority they go to their pulpits or their desks and brand as a *crime* an action which many people we honour and love have performed and deny an honourable burial to those who have departed this world voluntarily – since they cannot point to a single biblical authority, nor produce a single sound philosophical argument; it being made clear that what one wants are *reasons* and not empty phrases and abuse."[13]

Our anxiety, says Schopenhauer, arises out of the perpetual torment of the dictatorial Will to Live. All we have to do is to realize that, "To sleep is good; to die is better. Ah, but never to have been born – that is the secret!" Then we shall not be afraid to take our own lives. We must extinguish this tyrannical Will to Live which is the origin of all our sufferings. And we need not fear death: "But now, if after ten thousand years sleep, it was forgotten to wake you up, this would not, I think, be a very great misfortune since your period of non-being would have been so long compared with your brief period of being, you would have got quite used to it. What is certain, however, is that you would not have the least idea you had failed to be woken up."[14]

Unfortunately, we are not, I think, entirely convinced by Schopenhauer's attempts to reassure us. These seem to depend on our regarding death as a mere nonexistence. But what of "perchance to dream"? What of Stoppard's remark about not wanting to wake up and find yourself dead in a box? Doubts remain. Besides, Schopenhauer himself admits: "Perhaps there is no one alive who would not already have put an end to his life if this end were something purely negative, a sudden cessation of existence. But there is something positive in it as well: the destruction of the body. This is a deterrent, because the body is the physical form of the Will to Live." He might have added that there is also the fear of the pain involved in dying.

Alvarez reminds us that things are easier than they once were: "Modern drugs and domestic gas have not only made suicide more or less painless, they have also made it seem magical. A man who takes a knife and slices deliberately across his throat is murdering himself. But when someone lies down in front of an unlit gas fire, or swallows sleeping pills, he seems not so much to be dying as merely seeking oblivion for a while. In suicide, as in most other areas of activity, there has been a technological breakthrough which has made a cheap and relatively painless death democratically available to everyone."[15]

Suicide, like life itself, has its little ironies. A man decided to do away with himself, so he lay down in front of the unlit gas fire. However, it was North Sea gas, which does not contain carbon monoxide. He had also taken some sleeping pills. Not enough, apparently, for after a few hours he awoke. Thinking better of his original intention, he lit a cigarette. There was an explosion and he was killed. The North Sea gas, though non-toxic, is highly combustible.

It is a cliché to say that in our century we live "after the death of God" and that, as Nietzsche said, "After the death of God everything is permissible." Existentialist writers and other novelists in our own time have said that life is absurd and the only really important thing is human freedom as individually expressed. Suicide is therefore one of our options. It carries no moral stigma for the Absurdist. Indeed the reason for suicide does not even have to be profound or tragic: there is an account of an existentialist (a Surrealist poet) who shot himself outside a French café in the 1930s – *for a joke*!

Whatever writers say about the decline of civilizations and the neurotic or even absurd turn which our way of life has taken, most people do not live in perpetual panic because they cannot discover the Meaning of Life. Most people do however, endure dark moments and hours; and some kill themselves during such bad times. But most people manage to cheer up again, to learn to "take the rough with the smooth", to "count their blessings". Life's pleasures are measured against its pains. And there do seem to be things worth living for. Not many people would be entirely convinced by Schopenhauer's pessimistic saying: "Anyone who doubts the preponderance of pain over pleasure in this life has only to consider the sensations of an animal eating another animal, with the sensations of the animal being eaten." And the disagreeable nature – morally as well as physically – of the act of suicide is enough to deter most of us when the black moments assail us.

Besides, it seems to me that not all the arguments of the existentialists and the absurdists, the Kirilovs and those who would slaughter themselves over a glass of red wine are as convincing as they are sometimes assumed to be. Let us suppose that Kirilov is right when he says that the world is meaningless. He regards his suicide as an act of vengeance or rebellion. But against whom, or what? Not God, because a meaningless world can have no place for

God. It seems odd to try to avenge oneself against meaninglessness. What could such vengeance mean? Revenge only has meaning when it is against someone who can be expected to feel the force or pain of it. But revenge in a meaningless world is itself meaningless.

Let us suppose, again, that the world is absurd. Why should the act of taking voluntary leave of such a world carry more philosophical weight and stand as a sign of man's ultimate freedom when any number of alternative acts may be equally significant? In a meaningless world, what is it that is alleged to make suicide meaningful? Perhaps nothing. For in a meaningless world, all acts are equally meaningless. But the proposition, "Everything is meaningless" cannot be logically affirmed. Either it is true or it is false. If it is false, well then there is meaning in the world. If it is true, it is contradictory: for it is not possible *logically* to maintain that "Everything is meaningless" is meaningful. If everything is meaningless, then the proposition "Everything is meaningless" is also meaningless.

In fact, "meaninglessness" only has any sense when it can be contrasted with "meaningful" – when particular bits of meaninglessness can be set within the general context of meaning. Or, even if there is more meaninglessness about that meaning, there must be at least *some* meaning about in order that "meaninglessness" (as a word) can be meaningfully used. If it cannot be meaningfully used, then the world is not entirely meaningless. The argument is one of Necessary Contrast. The word "meaninglessness" relies on the existence of meaning just as the idea of counterfeit money depends upon the existence somewhere (in however small a quantity) of some genuine money.

Absurdism has had influence in a certain sort of

European philosophy and in modern novels and plays because of the determination of fashionable, chic intellectuals and critics and publishers to maintain its influence; and because there always seems to be a market among students and the next generation of writers for fashionable, chic despair. It is, after all, much easier to write about existential despair and meaninglessness, much more fun in a sort of vague pornographic sense to justify fantastically one's worst whims by writing of men and women wandering aimlessly in a world where there is no meaning, and hence no morals. Absurdism offers the writer or philosopher a spurious freedom from the difficult task of having to make decisions about right and wrong. And so we are back with Hamlet whose moral choices are obscured by his metaphysical darkness.

While we must admit the break-up of the medieval synthesis – what are the cathedrals now except monuments to a dead culture in which the blundering tourists gape at what they do not undestand? The *reality* of angels and heaven is no longer felt, and belief in them is, at best, only an intellectual idea – like the doctrine of transubstantiation. All these things can be upheld with intellectual integrity, but they are no longer part of our world: in Thomas Carlyle's poignant phrase, "They have receded from us."

So we admit the collapse of the grand design, of the last example in Europe of a coherent culture and world-view. All is now fragments and sects. But this does not lead to the supposition that everything is meaningless. Why should it be thought meaningless to build a bridge so that people may cross – if only to sit and enjoy a picnic on the other side? Why is it meaningless to feed the hungry? Because they will become hungry again, says the absurdist. And one day they will die. So – we shall all die one day: that does not imply there is nothing to live for. As Ezra Pound satirized the gloomy doctrines of A. E. Housman:

> O woe, woe,
> People are born and die,
> We also shall be dead pretty soon
> Therefore let us act as if we were dead already.[16]

Are Bach and Mozart meaningless? Is Shakespeare meaningless? If so, they are a lot less meaningless than those who waste their time, and ours, saying Woe, all is meaninglessness! Because meaning is limited, even scarce, we do not have to conclude that it does not exist. Meaning consists in order and form, in saying something that is not self-defeating and logically contradictory like "Everything is meaningless." Order and form – *and therefore meaning* – are supremely to be found in the masters of language and music whom we know as the great writers, painters and musicians. If anyone says, "Everything is meaningless" then he must agree that everything and Shakespeare, too, (apart from himself, the speaker) is meaningless. Now what sort of a person would say a damn fool thing like that! It is the essence of, say *Hamlet* that herein Shakespeare deals more meaningfully than anyone else has ever done in the modern world with the question of meaninglessness.

A true and practical existentialism appears however in the personal sense that "I" am meaningless, that my life has no purpose or significance. And this is a much more common cause of suicide than the general bleating about "the meaninglessness of the universe" and kindred vacuities. When we come to examine the actual incidence of suicide, we almost invariably find that the act was committed out of a particular and personal despair and disappointment, and not out of a disillusionment with the universe in general.

It maybe an unhappy love affair. Though it is disappointing for romantics to discover that more people (perhaps) killed themselves in America in 1929 because of the Wall Street crash, than on account of an insufferably bleeding heart. Poverty can provoke the extreme reaction. There is the pitiable case of Richard Smith, a tradesman who had fallen into debt, who, with his wife in 1732 determined on suicide, first killing their two-year-old child and then hanging themselves. They left a moving and highly-literate suicide-note in which they affirmed their belief in God and their love of his creation, but ". . . as we know the wonderful God to be Almighty, so we cannot help believing that he is also good – not implacable, but like such wretches as men are, not taking delight in the misery of his creatures . . . we were not idle or extravagant . . . we appeal to all who ever knew us, whether or not we have not taken as much pains to get our living as our neighbours, although not attended with the same success."

This act was not born out of philosophical conjecture of the fashionably negative kind. It reveals the depths of particular humans and particular miseries. Mental suffering, depression, sheer unhappiness produces suicides. The comedian Tony Hancock. The wonderfully talented musician David Munrow. The tortured novelist Malcom Lowry. Van Gogh. Why so many people of prodigious gifts do away with themselves is a dark mystery, but I believe it has something to do with an acute and persistent sensitivity which is also a sensitivity to darkness, to despair. It seems reasonable to believe that the light of creativity burns more brightly because it is set in a huge darkness. And it is no use recommending to a creative person who is profoundly unhappy that he take some comfort in past achievements: with creative artists, life is not like that. As W. H. Auden said, "Only the *next* poem matters." For the creative artist, nothing matters so much as his work. The story of Mozart feeling compelled to leave a banquet in order to sketch in a movement of a string quartet is exemplary. After a period spent in creation, there is some respite: but the ache and the compulsion return. It is this intolerable pressure which, I believe, finally drives so many creative artists to self-destruction: the insistent summons to creative endeavour and the appalling demands of the creative task – no one who has not felt at least something of this tension should think himself qualified to pronounce on the issue of the suicide of artists.

With some, the medical, pathological aspect is scarcely (if at all) veiled. So Virginia Woolf wrote to Leonard: "I fell certain that I am going mad again: I feel we can't go through another of those terrible times. And I shan't recover this time. I begin to hear voices and can't concentrate. So I am doing what seems the best thing to do . . ." She walked into the sea.

Her motive was to relieve Leonard and herself from anguish. It is not a bad desire: to wish to protect others, and especially those near us, from despair: ". . . I don't think two people could have been happier until this terrible disease came. I can't fight it any longer. I know that I am spoiling your life, that without me you could work. And you will, I know . . ."

Yet doubts remain. Why should a woman who could write, "You have given me the greatest possible happiness" and "I don't think two people could have been happier than we have been," say "I can't fight it any longer"? Were they really as happy as she tried to make out? There is something in, "I know that I am spoiling your life", "that without me you could work", and especially "*And you will I know*" which has an air of vengeance about it. Not vengeance on a meaningless world, but on an individual. Is there something in what she says – not all of it, by any means, but something – of, I told you you didn't appreciate me, so now I'm going, and it's *your* fault? No moral condemnation is applied to either side. It is clear from the rending, despairing tone of Virginia's letter that nothing was easy – the personal suffering involved was not something that could be weighed in any kind of utilitarian calculus. Suffering is suffering. And what people suffer cannot be measured by other people who look in from the outside. We do not know. Here, at least, is the place for reverent scepticism.

Anyone can be glib. There is an imperfect poem, a remote judgement of suicide by Vernon Scannell. It makes a point which we all recognize – that there is something in us all which wants to make our friends look at us, which wants them to see that we feel they have let us down. It objectifies disappointment as hatred:

> I wish that I was dead. Oh, they'll be sorry then.
> I hate them and I'll kill myself tomorrow.
> I want to die. I hate them, hate them. Hate.
>
> ". . . I want to die. I'll hurt them yet," he said,
> And once again: "I hate them, hate them." Hate.
> The lampless darkness roared inside his head,
> Then sighed into a silence in which played
> The grown-up voices, still up late,
> Indifferent to his rage as to his fate.[17]

It is easy enough to judge such an act as one of immaturity – "the grown-up voices" – but maybe those voices did not feel what the suicide felt. It is always a mistake to underestimate human feelings.

There are two main causes of suicides of this "chronic" variety. I say "chronic" in order to draw a distinction between suicide which is the truly rash act, accomplished in sudden anger or remorse and suicide as the culmination of years of self-destruction. The first cause is the sensation of being unloved: its archetypal expression is in the poem by Malcolm Lowry, *Where Has Tenderness Gone?* And the second, not unrelated, cause is self-hate. Not unrelated because – "If I find myself unlovable, how can anyone else love me, no matter what they *say*?"

Are such suicides immature? Is it childish, among all things in this life, to want to be loved by those we love? To want some feeling of human warmth and *lasting* affection? And to wonder, when these things do not appear: where has tenderness gone?

A close friend of mine did himself in. He had been a lonely homosexual, highly intelligent, a gifted musician – though not conventionally attractive. "Rather squat and run to fat." While he was alive and taking refuge from "the slings and arrows" in very heavy drinking, a mutual friend – not an unsympathetic man – said to me, "He'd be OK, you know, Geoffrey; there's lots of blokes who'd give him his fun for a night. But the trouble with Geoffrey is that he wants a permanent relationship." The *trouble*! As Lowry said, "Where has tenderness gone?"

Because Geoffrey was unloved, he felt himself to be unlovable. So, unlovable as he felt, he hated himself. Hating himself, he gave himself over to much that was squalid and unworthy of his talents; to pornography and alcoholism. Vicious acts of self-indulgence which are more accurately described as even more vicious acts of self-denial; that is denial of his true, lovable and valuable self. For he was kind. It was not a dramatic suicide. A death through natural causes, in fact; and within the clinical respectability of the hospital. But I knew it was suicide, really. Fifteen years of loneliness and self-hate. Too many bottles of whisky. Too much auto-eroticism. This gifted, kind teacher – what he wanted was affectionate companionship and not a one-night stand. Where has tenderness gone?

So – if one may still quote Scripture in a godless century – "Thou shalt love thy neighbour as thyself." Like all the great moral phrases in the Bible, this is not a bland directive but a summary of psychological-spiritual truth. It is like the last line in a beautiful theorematic proof; full of subtlety, containing in short space a whole argument, a long story. Q.E.D. The issue is the relationship between self-love and love of the other. Important themes running alongside are (1) the difference between selfishness and true self-love, and (2) whether one can love at all without first having experienced what it is like to be loved.

The New Testament issues what many preachers treat as a directive: "Thou shalt love thy neighbour as thyself" – do this *or else*! Also, if we know how to read it, it gives us the answer to the insoluble problem about love: "Herein is love, not that we loved God, but that he loved us, and sent his Son to be the propitiation for our sins."[18]

Whatever else those words are – in a metaphysical or in a supernatural sense – they are first of all a description of psychological reality: you *cannot* love unless you have experienced love. The Bible tells us that we are loved, that God himself loves us. But how can we know this? The Tourist Board has turned the Father's House into a den of thieves. Bishops, anxious to be loved by radical feminists, publicly despise Our Mother. Sins, which, according to St John, love propitiates, are taken to be nonexistent. "Christ" is either the name of a cosmic conjurer or else a swearword – depending on whether you take your linguistic guidance from the charismatic movement or the taproom.

To be told from a great height, the height of biblical authority no less, is useless unless you can feel loved. George Eliot again: "No one ever heard the divine pity, except by lips that were moved by human pity." Blake said:

> To Mercy, Pity, Peace and Love
> All pray in their distress.
> For Mercy has a human heart,
> Pity a human face,
> And Love, the human form divine,
> And Peace, the human dress.[19]

"And love the human form divine." What, a society wedding? And Geoffrey sitting in a filthy room – head and heart full of gifts – drinking himself to death in a condition of chronic self-hate? Where has tenderness gone? What solution is there to this problem except the sacrament of despair, suicide? I am unlovable; so no one loves me. So I cannot love. Because I cannot love, I despise myself. The more I despise myself – and this is what happened in Geoffrey's case – the more I let myself sink. So the musicianship was neglected, the intellectual brilliance turned only to massively insightful acts of self-denigration, the house stinking; an empty whisky bottle – another bottle.

Deliver us not into the bitter pains of eternal death.

There is, must be, another biblical word on this intractable issue. There is: "Love thine enemy." And who or what is the enemy? It is a sharper form of the earlier commandment, "Love thy neighbour as thyself." Thyself is the enemy. Loving thine enemy is loving thyself. The enemy is all the faults and weaknesses of our character – faults real or imagined, usually both, fantasized upon, burnished into a false self-image. The enemy, the Devil, the Father of Lies. The inward part of myself which tells me, lying, I am *only* my faults. "The invisible worm that flies in the night."

This false self-image feeds the feeling that I am unlovable. It oozes guilt and self-disgust. It encourages a squalid life of self-neglect and self-destruction. It breeds suicide. I am no good – best done away with.

But it is a *false* self-image. It is a lie. There is, under all the dirt, a part of us which is wholesome and creative – something to which our being tends, the goal of our development and the definition of our maturity. This is the true self who must be loved before we can love our neighbour as ourself. Because this part of us is the deepest and most wholesome part, it is able to help us overcome self-disgust and self-loathing. "Herein is Love, not that we loved God, but that he loved us." The mature, wholesome, unconscious, unrealized but nonetheless real, deep part of ourself is the image of God within us. Notice what God, literally and psychologically does: He sends, "His Son to be a propitiation for our sins".

And in human terms, in the terms of what is actually felt in a lived life, this "Son" is our fraught and anxiety-stricken ego; consciousness despising ourself, making false images of ourself – false gods. "He was despised and rejected, a man of sorrows and acquainted with grief." This suffering, self-despising consciousness must atone, come to terms with the enemy. To love thyself. To love the part of thyself which is the enemy. To translate myth into practical reality, this means that there is an aspect of our being – the deepest aspect – which can love us warts and all: love us not in spite of our faults, but love us unconditionally. This is redemption, the great reconciliation. And it is not something which takes place only in myth and religious poetry – though it does take place there – but in our own self, this too solid flesh. We have the power to free ourselves from suicidal self-hate and the delusion of unlovableness. The only way is by learning to love the enemy within.

This does not mean excusing our faults, or of trying to deny even that we have any faults. It means, first of all, recognizing our faults, weaknesses and vices for what they are: the reverse side of our virtues and strengths. For virtues and vices are opposites only in the sense that two sides of a coin are opposites. The vice is only the negative side of the virtue. This is unavoidable: a bright light casts a dark shadow. A man may be brilliantly intelligent and quick-witted. The dark side of this virtue may be that he is impatient with more pedestrian types, does not suffer fools gladly. A man may be something of a waster or spendthrift. At the same time he may display conspicuous generosity. And so it is with all the vices and virtues.

I do not mean to define virtues and vices according to a strict moral code, but only to decribe virtues as creative dispositions and vices as destructive ones. The task is to turn the enemy into the friend, to use the energy we put into destruction (and particularly self-destruction) into creativity and what builds up: to turn the vices into virtues. It is in this creative, psychological sense that Aristotle made his famous remark about virtue (*aretē*) and happiness (*eudaimonia*): "Only the virtuous are happy." It might be more picturesquely translated: "Only those who aim at the true centre (for Aristotle the Golden Mean) are possessed by the Easy Demon." We go out of our way, when we are feeling self-destructive, to be possessed by the tortuous, uneasy demon.

The image of God within us which is the self whom we must learn to love before we can love our neighbour as ourself, is the deep, unconscious resource of personality which can reconcile the warring factions which are also within us. This is the deep, unconscious, undiscovered wholesomeness which is there, working all the time to make us whole: to use the language of biblical myth, this is the God who loved us before we loved him.

The fraught and anxiety-stricken ego, full of despising and grief, must become subject before the deeper forces within the personality: "The Father is greater than I." Both sides of the coin are made by the mint. The suffering, self-despising ego and the enemy are but surface eruptions of a psychological-spiritual complexity which works for our good, for our integration, and at a much deeper level. This is the level of reconciliation.

The typical suicidal personality sees only the black. He only hates himself. Of course, he will project this hatred, saying that what he really hates is the world, or the flesh or the devil – or the local borough council. (And there may be grounds for such hatreds!) But deep calleth unto deep, and what the depths are always working for is the integration of the enemy.

As in the chapter on bereavement, so now, it is necessary to make a stern but realistic judgement. And it is this: sometimes the forces of reconciliation from within fail. As we do not "cope with" a bereavement, so, perhaps, we do not manage to resist casting ourselves into the suicidal abyss. It is regrettable, but it has to be said – because this is the way things are, and it is no service to God or man to pretend that every story has a happy ending. I shall say more about this in the last chapter.

But such depths of human misery! There are people

who kill themselves in loneliness and poverty, assailed by debts and frustrated in love. There are also many who make away with themselves surrounded by the kindness of friends – or who have walked away from the bliss of loving and love, sensual, tender, indubitable, only to throw themselves under a train. For whatever reason?

Material life, economic life proceeds on the assumption of "if . . . then". Buy cheap and sell expensive, if you can. There is a sort of Karma of material reward: if you deal circumspectly, providentially, you will gain your reward. It so often turns out the reward is money, and woes which not even money can assuage form another sort of tragedy: the petty tragedy (no less for being petty) of earnest souls who have put their trust in sound finance, and a not altogether unenjoyed going-without; but who now come to their old age full of bitterness and disillusion; mean-spirited, despite themselves. And this is a kind of death, or living-death.

Psychological-spiritual life does not work according to the same economy. A rich man – or one merely aspiring to make a few thousand pounds – knows about interest rates, follows his stocks and shares in the daily paper and can more or less predict the outcome of his investments, make adjustments when necessary and all the rest. But in the world of human feeling there is no similar calculus of investments. I come back to David Munrow, a young, prodigiously talented musician, handsome, with a life of music-making before him – with a devoted lover – and he does himself in. And the nasty little man with his little investments survives this run on the pound, this increase in interest-rates – as if these were the things that matter.

Perhaps he is right. But what is he compared with David Munrow or Van Gogh?

But he does not want to be anything to compare with

them. He "admires" rather than appreciates their talent. These artists are, of course, great geniuses, but their doings must not be allowed to interfere with real life – the trappings of investment.

"You cannot serve God and Mammon."

And the irony is that the mammonish petty investor and provident-miser believes he has God on his side. There is something about rectitude that is repulsive. And he regards the artist – I mean the real thing not the superannuated dilettantes who pick up the Arts Council subsidies – as a luxury, somebody or something to be indulged when he has got home from the counting-house: but only indulged if the art is fashionable. He is petty bourgeois and it is the petty bourgeoisie who have defined suicide as a sin.

There are bereavements which go unreconciled, men and women comfortless. There is no mere technique for solving these issues. So, in the question of suicide, there are some people who are victims, whom nothing can help – technique least of all. I think it has to be admitted, against the great cloud of well-doers and kind-thinkers, that, for a few people, suicide may be the only way to proceed – and therefore to admit that it may be the right way to proceed.

To say these things is heresy, of course. But heresy with mercy is to be preferred to callous orthodoxy. If there is nothing that can be done to ease someone's chronic misery, who are we to insist that he must go on suffering it – we who do not comprehend a half of what he is going through? Many, perhaps most, woes can be alleviated, but there are some which cannot be relieved. Some stories end unhappily: that is the meaning of tragedy, the supreme manifestation of art in the history of our civilization from the days of Sophocles. And in a tragedy, the best motives, the most luminous intelligences and even selfless goodwill and charity are overwhelmed by circumstances or fate. The tragic hero dies an undeserved death. So in the case of the suicide, the apportioning of blame and the strict moral line which makes taking one's own life cowardly and sinful should be rejected. We never know the whole story behind another person's suffering. Judgement, therefore, is presumptuous and arrogant. And it would be a callous person who refused an easier death to someone suffering from, say, one of the worst forms of terminal cancer.

Unhappy people – the so-called "mentally ill" – and suicides are, in a sense, victims who suffer as they do on behalf of the rest of us an extreme of life's terrors and tensions. A great number of fairly ordinary folk have done away with themselves because they were in debt or disgrace, in the throes of some nameable crisis. But many enormously talented and intelligent people have gone the same way. What was the nature of a sensitivity as acute as Van Gogh's which led him to see life with the eyes of artistic genius but then to put an end to that life?

There are depths of horror. No one who has not known the unnameable torment involved in merely surviving the next ten seconds has any right to assume a lofty disdain of suicide. There does not have to be anything conventionally "wrong" in the life and experience of the suicide. The mystery of self-destruction is one of the deepest of all mysteries. Recently, a prisoner killed himself by hanging in his cell in a northern prison. The prison Medical Officer – who was also a psychiatrist – had seen him a few hours before the suicide. His remarks are instructive, in a sense, though there is no lessening of the mystery: "Of all the men in jail, I would have thought him the least likely to attempt suicide. He radiated bonhomie. He seemed to be at peace with himself."

This sensitivity is often called madness merely because it is not usual, and we have no other word for what we do not understand. Sensitivity reveals the depths, and in those depths there are unspeakable joys – and woes. The classic description of these psychological deeps is to be found in our fairy stories where the opposites of bliss and terror are portrayed in the figures of beautiful princesses, golden harps, golden hinds and witches, giants, blood and decapitation. These tales are, of course, irrational. So is life, and no less terrifying for that. We all know something of the excitement and terror of the fairy tale or the ghost story. Then we put down the book, make a homely pot of tea and fill in the income-tax form before retiring to bed. Imagine what it must feel like to live in that world of numinous stories without relief. This is part of what I mean when I say that mad people, visionary poets and suicides are victims and that somehow they suffer on behalf of the rest of us things which we are neither permitted nor condemned to see for ourselves.

> . . . the backward half-look
> Over the shoulder towards the primitive terror.

The world of the fairy tale. Acute reality. The unbearable, holy and terrifying experience of existence itself. Great art arises out of an awareness of these things. Great art is therefore, because it is "deep calling unto deep", a help to us all when we have to cope with an encounter with what is truly disturbing. How many dark nights survived by listening to Schubert's *Death and the Maiden* string quartet! But think what it must have cost Schubert to write it, to have lived in depths so deep.

The suicide often feels radical disorientation in the world and this is unbearable if it persists. So Celia in *The Cocktail Party* says:

Well, there are two things I can't understand,
Which you might consider symptoms. But first I must
   tell you
That I should really *like* to think there's something
   wrong with me –
Because, if there isn't, then there's something wrong,
Or at least, very different from what it seemed to be,
With the world itself – and that's much more
   frightening!
That would be terrible. So I'd rather believe
There is something wrong with me . . .[20]

The price paid for artistic vision is suffering which can become intolerable: to have entered those depths. The suicide then is an expiatory victim, for he goes into those depths and brings out emotional treasures which sustain us and give a sense of perspective when we are called upon to endure merely a whiff of the horrors. Where would our nights be without *Hamlet*, without Mozart?

But it is not only a question of high art. Western civilization and culture is really formed by three historical experiences: Judaism, Christianity and the Ancient Greeks – particularly Greek philosophy and tragedy. All three cultural experiences are approaches to the problem of human suffering. The Jews of the Old Testament were, as a Rabbi once said to me, "Not so much chosen as singled-out". It is a story told over and again of slavery and exile. The rites and ceremonies are full of suffering images: the Scapegoat, the Suffering Servant and the need for Atonement. The poetry, also, reaches the heights and depths of contemplation in the Book of Job which is the story of innocent suffering.

One Greek philosophical school after another tries to give an answer to the question, Why suffering? And the

Greek drama, especially in Sophocles, is built round this issue. The drama was a mixture of theatre and liturgy. When the citizens turned out to watch the tragedies, they also participated, were meant to be sent home purged and cleansed. The word for cleansing, "catharsis", had its beginning in the ritual dramas of the polis.

Christianity, of course, is built on the crucified victim. Not just Jesus in the New Testament, but the crucifix in stone, wood and glass in a thousand years of European art. And not only the cosmic Christ in agony, but his mother, Stabat Mater Dolorosa.

Judaism, the Greeks and Christianity agree on one thing: there is no solution to the problem of evil in any theoretical or even theological sense. It simply has to be lived through. But they give us a way of living through it. They offer the images and icons of suffering humanity as marks of solidarity. We are all in it together. The Jews were, are, a people. Nationhood. "By the waters of Babylon, we sat down and wept . . . how shall we sing the Lord's song in a strange land?" And at the individual level suffering is a mystery. It is beyond us. "Where wast thou when I laid the foundations of the earth?" And "Canst thou draw out Leviathan with a fish-hook?" – these are the answers which God gives to suffering, speculative Job out of the whirlwind. Of course, they are no answers at all, but only repetitions of the central truth that suffering is a mystery.

The New Testament goes further and, by the doctrine of the Incarnation in which God empties himself and becomes one of us, suggests that God as well is in the same case as mankind: he cannot answer the problem of suffering except by suffering.

And so we approach the truth that all suffering is somehow redemptive, that in some way,

All shall be well
And all manner of thing shall be well.

There is nothing glib about this. It is a comfort to be inferred directly from the stories of suffering in those three strands of our historical tradition. The exiled, enslaved and dispossessed Jews also had a vision of a restored Kingdom, a Messianic Banquet and a final assize in which what is presently insoluble will be solved. The Greeks knew catharsis, the here and now resolution of the problem of suffering in the real life of the individual. Christianity presents the cross, the union of the opposites, the horizontal line of human life and suffering intersected by the vertical line of God's judgement – which is also, besides being a sign of final reckoning, a reminder of the beginning: Incarnation.

In my end is my beginning.[21]

It is not just the case that we crave to be redeemed from our suffering but, as all that is deepest in the history of our culture shows, the suffering itself is redemptive. And that is why, beyond any narrow judgement about suicide as an affront to God, the torment of those who are driven to make away with themselves is not finally pointless, wasted.

The whole of experience shows that there has to be suffering. Only we do not know why, quite. It seems to be bound up with growth and maturing. Individual cases – and not only the lives of the saints – reveal this truth. Of all the experiences which develop and make a man, it seems again and again that his pain and how he deals with it is the most formative, crucial. All our protests that life *should not* be arranged in this way pale before the reality: this is how things are. If you doubt it, read Aeschylus, Job, Sophocles and St Mark's Gospel. What of the Pieta or the

Miserere, the war-graves and the Requiem?

The torments of those inclined to suicide, and especially of those who actually do the deed, are also redemptive. There is no *noble* suffering and *ignoble* suffering. It is all one. Humanity is a generic term and we are all in the same boat. Pain is a necessity. Education involves suffering. No French without tears. Piano lessons! The eight times table. Punctuation and spelling. Pain is built into the way things are, and there is not much use grumbling at the fact – as Job found out.

If, even in small matters like moderate literacy and semi-competent musicianship, some element of suffering is unavoidable, how much more should we expect it to be a part of our final wholeness – what St Paul calls, "The glory that shall be revealed in us"? Well, he spells it out for us: "The whole creation groaneth and travaileth in pain *together*", "waiting the adoption, to wit, the redemption of our body". The solidarity is in that "together". No man is an island.

The self-hate and perplexity that leads some of us to suicide is also part of the indivisibility which is redemptive suffering.

"Death, Thou Shalt Die": Coping

One short sleep past, we wake eternally,
And death shall be no more; death, thou shalt die.[1]

These are lines from a powerful poem by John Donne. Can you believe them? Does the resurrection to eternal life have any power to convince us in the age of secularism and science, of materialism and refined agnosticism?

Perhaps there is no resurrection. Maybe the belief that we rise again is only primitive and unschooled, something which in our day has become reduced to mere wishful thinking. This may be so. But there is a glibness about contemporary scepticism. I would not even go so far as to give it the title of "scepticism". For scepticism, doubt – as we noticed in Descartes – requires thought, very rigorous thought. Much present unbelief arises not out of thought at all, but out of the fashionable pseudo-scientific clichés in favour of atheism; and out of unthought prejudices which characterize what has come to be known as "studio-debate".

The first of these "unthoughts" is that science has somehow disproved religion and rendered it meaningless. What "meaningless" means here, of course, is simply "old-fashioned" – something that "We", glued to the soppy-sensational television science programmes, have no time for. The reasons for scepticism are rarely examined on television. Indeed, it is a matter of some doubt whether, given the way the TV debate is rigged (not to be "too deep", not to be "too academic", but to be seen to give space to every opinion, however quirky, however stupid; not to be seen to come to any "definite conclusion" because that may cause people to think that the ordinary rules of logic were greater than the egalitarianism of the Producer), matters of religious belief and scepticism can be discussed at all on TV except in a form which renders them anodyne.

What of this belief that science has disproved or superseded religion? It is mere fashion and nothing else. Somehow it has come to be assumed that words like "soul" and "God" are archaic and suspect, that they do not point to anything definite or true any more. It is sort of assumed – even by the mass of folk who know nothing of science and still less of religion – that Darwin's monkeys, a few incomprehensible remarks by Einstein tacked on to space-probes and the ubiquitous microchip (who said, "chips with everything"?) have made God and the religious outlook redundant. Even the Church sometimes seems to half-believe this modern superstition which I shall call the doctrine of Technological Barbarism.

For thousands of years mankind has believed that he possesses an immortal soul. It was not only so-called "primitive" people who believed this but Plato. Is Plato not deemed to be as intelligent as the Producer of *Tomorrow's World* or *QED*? It is the superstition of microscopes, X-rays and telescopes which has done away with our confidence in our immortality. When Gagarin first orbited the earth, the Russians jibed, "He didn't find God up there!" It is not a question of Plato disproved, but of Plato unfashionable. The spirit of the age has its own reasons, though perhaps "reason" is not quite the right word, for disbelieving in the immortality of the soul. And so it appeals to "the facts of science" to provide a phoney intellectual credibility for what are really no more than prejudices.

Christian theologians did not believe that the soul is "in" the body, as if it were an organ or tissue of the body. The main reason for the concept of a soul at all is in order to distinguish what is physical from what is spiritual. "The soul" is a spiritual concept, not a ghost in the machine. It is meant to refer to individual character and personality, the principle of individuation, what makes you, you, and me, me. This individuating principle was perceived as unique in every case. None of us is exactly alike. The means of expressing this uniqueness was to talk of "soul". St Paul when he preaches the resurrection of the dead is not so foolish as to imagine he is talking about the reconstitution of rotted corpses: he speaks of the *soma-pneumaticon* – the spiritual body.

In other words, Paul was talking of two sorts of being, and of two realms: a physical realm and a spiritual realm. If we wish to say what Paul was saying in the newer understanding of our own day, we could say he was talking about two languages, two ways of talking: one about natural science and the other about religion. Much contemporary scepticism, unthought, is a conflation of bifocal ignorance: ignorance of science and religion alike.

It is highly instructive to note, in passing, that the only time in the history of western civilization when the location of the soul was a problem, was in Descartes – the very thinker who invented and perpetuated the mind-body split. Descartes located the soul in the penial gland, the "third eye" of truly primitive superstition.

Popular pseudo-science assumes that we are no more than our bodily parts and that therefore we *cannot* in any sense be imagined as living on after the death of the body. But a biologically-based, scientific-materialist way of speaking about human beings is inadequate. We know this because all attempts to speak of people as "organisms" and to describe our lives in terms of "behaviour" and "conditioned reflexes" does not do justice to our own sense of life at its deepest. It is no use trying to dismiss a person's abiding depression by telling him it is "really" only an imbalance of chemicals in his brain. It is no good describing being in love as, "a disorder of affect". Our too solid frame is more than a bag of numbers.

The medico-scientific orthodoxy chiefly promulgated by television documentaries is antihuman. Its attempt to explain human nature in terms of "ducts", "glands", "amino-acids" and all the rest, is yet one more lapse from the picture to the diagram.

> Grimmer than Freud
> And not half so romantic,
> Stood the Experimental psychologist;
> Brave Behavourist,
> Measurer, Quantifier,
> Brain bulging, and Factor Analysis providing
> A million different answers for
> Questions we never ask.
> And, should he tell you he has fallen in love,
> Do not believe him, unless he can give you
> The accurate angle of inclination
> And the quantifiable impact of the fall.

That verse needs no citation, for I wrote it myself in desperation at the antihuman performance of the Psychology Department when I was studying that subject at university. I had gone in for psychology because, naive as we are when young, I had thought the subject might enhance my understanding of human nature and so help to assuage my general curiosity and also be useful to me as a priest. I found it to be a mere caricature of human experience, a nonsense of befogging, blinding insight's eyes with jargon and pseudo-expertise; inventing its own terminology in which to misdescribe real problems of human experience for which poets and novelists had already discovered the proper words.

It is all a sham, a superstition. It is a pseudo-intellectual way of airing one's antireligious prejudices. It is really an excuse for idleness, the preference for a formula approved by all the fashionable people instead of taking the trouble to look at the real masters of human psychology: St Paul, Augustine, Pascal, Kierkegaard and the others. In passing, again, it is worth reminding ourselves that "Psychology" – this word usurped by the Behavourists and Mechanics who run the university departments – means "study of the soul". How dare they steal a good word! They do not even believe in the mind, let alone the soul.

Now, this is the crux: if the spirit of the age, as expressed by television documentaries, the declined academic professions and gloomy books "to accompany the TV Series", cannot tell us the truth about us when we are alive, why should we believe what they have to predict on the subject of what follows or does not follow our death? If they do not understand earthly things, why should we believe them when they tell us there is no heaven?

In Christian theology, the resurrection of the body means that the death of our physical members is not the end of us. But, as we have noticed, it is only the pseudo-scientific prejudiced types of the present age who believe that the resurrection of the body means putting back the youthful flesh on rotted (or crematorially evanesced) corpses. We have looked at the doctrine of the resurrection in the language and thought of St Paul and understood him rightly to mean that the resurrection of the body means the restoration or the reconstitution of the whole personality – the *soma-pneumaticon* – after the terrible event of death.

This *soma-pneumaticon* (it hardly needs to be said) is an extension and a development of the doctrine of the Incarnation: mind and body together. Thought and action together. Idea and reality together – as we have seen brilliantly exemplified in the medieval cathedrals, in the thought that we see man as a whole being, body and mind together; in all the religious language derived from the great realization of the truth: "The Word was made flesh." In other words, reason and stuff, substance, are inextricably joined. That is why the doctrine of immortality in the Christian, incarnational, tradition is described as the resurrection of a body: there is some persistence of substance and not of mere ideas.

So what I want above all to emphasize is that there really is no good reason for rejecting the doctrine of resurrection – no reason, at least from the outpourings of Technological Barbarism.

There is also, for our encouragement, the biblical story. And the main part of this encouragement is, paradoxically, to be found in all the depressing things which the Bible says about mankind: that we are fickle, faithless and fallen creatures, vile bodies and miserable sinners. We know, to our shame, that all of this is true. Well, if the scriptures are so right about us in such depths, why should we mistrust them when they tell us of our heights? It is exactly the opposite of what applied in the case of contemporary Technological Barbarism. Because the scriptures *do* accurately describe to us earthly things, we can trust them when they tell us of heaven.

There is no good argument out of Technological Barbarism against the resurrection of the dead and the life of the world to come. And there are many arguments in its favour, for instance:

(i) The biblical promises
(ii) The Greek philosophers' idea of our immortality
(iii) Evolution

The third argument is interesting. Any true doctrine of evolution does not refer to what might happen according to mindless chance. It is also a doctrine of development. A creature strives towards its goal, its purpose, its final cause or meaning – in Aristotle's word, its *telos*. We do not know what this *telos* is, still less how to achieve it. "We see through a glass darkly." And, as Jung said, most of our progress towards any degree of wholeness is largely unconscious. "What we are, that we know; what we shall be, it doth not yet appear."

Telos is hierarchical. As the grass exists for the cow; and the cow for man; so man exists for God: "to praise Him and glorify Him forever". The analogy from the world of – if I may use an arrogant phrase – "lesser creatures", applies to us also. Everything is for something. Nothing is for nothing. So what are we for? For God – "to praise Him and to enjoy Him for all eternity".

We still have to go through this disjunction of dying and death. The doctrine of eternal life is helpful, but even those whom it helps are not thereby freed from death's terrors. The only people who do not fear death are fanatics. However, there are some who are not comforted by the doctrine of eternal life, and it is worthwhile to spend some space on their considerably deeper objection to life after death than that of the Technological Barbarians.

This is the argument that the resurrection to eternal life solves nothing. For I am in relationship here on earth with others. These relationships involve joy and pleasure certainly, but they also involve pain and sadness. This is the way life is. There are no doubt bits of it for which I am truly thankful and other bits which I could wish improved. But *this* is the way things are. And I am created by my relationships. My life is a history of interactions with others, and these interactions have made me what I am. And this, I suppose, inferring my argument from what has happened to me in the past and also from my observation of people much older than myself, is how things will continue until I die.

What then?

"One short sleep past, we wake eternally," says Donne. And to what do we awake? If it is to more of the same – more and more and more stretching out to infinity – then the exercise would seem to some to be self-limiting, boring even. Do we really want *this* for ever and ever? Joy and woe, work and rest, the perpetual cauldron of significance bubbling along with trivialities. This infinity would be to some infinitely tedious. They argue that such an eternal life, were it to exist, solves nothing because it is not desirable. It would become a worse hell than all the caricatured demons of sub-Christian iconography.

But what if it is not like this? What if, instead, God wipes away all tears from our eyes and there is an end to pain and woe? Suppose we enter, after death, a state of permanent bliss? But I am not used to this. I am what I am as a product of the sort of life and relationships which involve pain and woe as well as joy and pleasure. The meaning of "life" for all of us is how we cope with and adjust to difficulties as well as how we enjoy our delights. We are the creatures of particular experience. We are the sum of relationships and reflections upon those relationships. Interactions and adjustments. Some good and successful, and others less good – even tragic.

Remove all the difficulties from a relationship and you radically alter the relationship. Lovers rejoice when they are reunited precisely because they have been parted. We enjoy food because we have been hungry. We sleep because we have been tired. It follows that, if you keep the partings, the hunger and the tiredness forever, then you will have an infinity of what we have now. If you, or God, wipe away all tears and leave only permanent bliss, then you radically alter the nature of the person who is transported to the state of bliss. In order for *me* to enjoy eternal life, I should have to be recognizably (to myself and selfconsciousness) *me*. But to take away the half of what has gone to create me means that *I* as *I* am myself thereby uncreated.

It is not just that the world of eternal bliss would be different from my present experience and that I should have to get used to it. It is rather that *I* would not be *I* in such a world. And, if the argument about the consolations of the life to come is to have any effect, it seems necessary that the identity and selfconsciousness of the person remains the same on both sides of the grave. If it is not *I* – the *I* of all my experienced relationships – who is resurrected, then the doctrine of resurrection is meaningless. What usually goes unnoticed in the arguments about the consolation of the life of the world to come is that the life there portrayed and envisaged is so radically different (e.g. entirely blissful or utterly hellish) that it would not, and could not, be described as a continuation of the life which *I* as *I*, or *you* as *you*, was living here on earth.

Human life demands the tensions of pain and pleasure, of anticipation and realization, or longing and consummation. This is, by the way, one of the reasons why music is pleasing: it proceeds from discord to concord, from imperfection to resolution. We wait for the dissonance to be resolved on the major (or minor) triad. Music is a sound-picture of our experience.

So the religious images of heaven and hell are not meant to be taken literally, for heaven and hell are not really separable: they are aspects of what it is to be human. Once again, our language is our teacher. It is necessarily binary and dualistic. "Happiness" can be defined, used as a real word to name a real experience, only if "pain" also names a reality. "Satisfaction" is understandable only where there is the possibility of dissatisfaction. That is to say, heaven exists in necessary contradiction and permanent experiential partnership with hell. If all that is changed, if the language we use to describe what human life *is* becomes so radically altered, then *we* are not *we* any more. The *I* that is resurrected would not be *me*. We think and act according to certain language-based distinctions. Abolish the distinctions by creating afterlives of hell and heaven and you abolish all that is meant by *us*.

This means that heaven and hell as separate and posthumous states necessarily cannot exist for *us*. It does not, however, abolish them as present realities; only it properly describes them as moral, emotional and religious aspects, polarities in one whole. The whole is life, and it is the only life which *we* as *we* can live. The afterlife could, of course, be something entirely new, a complete remaking of personality. But a *complete* remaking would not be a remaking, only a new creation. Sometimes the

Bible seems to take this view too: "Behold I make all things new."

These arguments show clearly that we cannot escape from the constraints of our language. If a proposition can be revealed as self-contradictory – because of the internal logic and meaning of words – then that proposition cannot be reasonably held. What happens in ordinary, everyday unreflective life is so often, as Wittgenstein said, "the bewitchment of our intelligence by the misuse of language". Language has developed to account for our experiences. There is no other way of expressing or of defining these experiences – however deep, however shallow – except by language. Only the most muddle-headed Logical Positivist would see this truth as a restriction. Was Shakespeare restricted? Plato? Mozart?Our language works as it does because it is the culmination and distillation of our experience. So if we look closely at it, we shall not be restricted or reduced: because it is the distillation of our experience, it has secrets to teach us. Wittgenstein again: "Create a language and you create a world." The rejection of these arguments, or of arguments in general, as "only words" betrays a misunderstanding of the true status of language. The Word was made flesh. We cannot experience the world without naming its parts. The first thing we want to know of any new and surprising thing is what it is called. As wrestling Jacob said to God, "Tell me thy name."

The close attention to how we use language can lead us out of naive error and dispel many neurotic fears. Neurosis is, in fact, language gone wrong: even the psychiatrists admit this in a tacit way when they call the phobias "irrational" fears. So the fact that our language excludes for *us* both heaven and hell as posthumous eternities, does not imply the end of metaphysical speculation, and, in particular, speculation about the meaning of "time".

If we were not before we arrived, and if we shall not be after we have departed, then our lives are strictly, logically, eternal. Because we were not before we were born and because we shall not be after we have died, we cannot in either of those states be said to be experiencing time. But to be is necessarily to experience time. That is to say, time is for each of us subjective. It begins when we are born and ends when we die. "Don't worry," as Schopenhauer or/and Stoppard might have said, "there's no danger that you'll wake up and find yourself dead!"

A conscious death is a contradiction in terms – i.e. in language.

It follows that "eternal life" means "life"; and life is life as we understand it, as we live it. However, neither an ill thought-out, propositionally-misconceived notion of eternal life as something that comes after death, nor of recognition that "eternity" (time being subjective) only has meaning while we are alive does anything – except perhaps among the most disembodied intellects – to dispel the fear of death. What does the fear of death really consist in, then? That, and not vague supernaturalism and the contradictions of speculative mataphysics, is the question of this last chapter. That is *the* question.

The fear of death arises directly out of the fact that we are conscious of death. I do not believe that the animals fear it. They avoid it when they can, and there is some evidence to show that they accept it when it becomes inevitable. But they do not agonize. Human beings do agonize. Death is the end of life: a banality. But it is also the beginning of life – it is *the* fact under which all that is great in life is created. Without the consciousness of impending death in the life of Shakespeare we could not have *Hamlet*. Some of our greatest music is in the Requiem. We do as we do because we are as we are. And without the awareness of death we should not be as we are, but something else. Time begins with my birth and it ends with my death. What happens in the interim is sometimes wonderfully enriching; moreover it is born of death. Our consciousness of death is the spirit which drives our art and motivates our morality. It is only the awareness of death which makes self-sacrifice a moral possibility. Our lives are lived, then, under the reality of death and our greatest achievements could not be shaped without it. Why then do we fear death and regard it as an evil? How to cope?

We fear death because it seems to be a restriction. Yet we can imagine infinity, talk about infinity and even use it in mathematical calculations. Part of us feels that, though we do not go on for ever, we ought to go on for ever. And the foregoing arguments about the nature of time – while they may be acceptable to our thoughts – are not acceptable to our feelings. We feel there will be a time when we are dead. This does not mean anything, for being dead means there is no "we" and no "time" either. Logical enough, but still our emotions are disturbed. As Stoppard said, "You wouldn't like to wake up and find yourself dead in a box, would you?"

Logic does not dispel our fear of death any more than it drives out our love of life. Feelings go deeper and arguments and feelings are attached to specific times, places and actions. Love poetry, for instance, always has something of death about it, as the lover – it may be by the stream in springtime – is driven to ponder that "This, too, even this will pass." It is no use saying to him, "Don't worry, you won't be there to regret its passing: you'll be safely dead, into non-being, out of time . . ." His feelings say differently. It seems outrageous to him that *this* should ever end.

So, part of our fear of death is caused by the fact that it reveals our deepest relationships, our strongest loves and most exquisite apprehensions of beauty as finite. A grievous blow to human beings who can imagine infinity. Surely it is out of this feeling, and not out of metaphysical speculation, that we have been driven in all ages to describe the world as meaningless? It was particular experiences which led Hamlet to exclaim:

> How weary, stale, flat and unprofitable
> Seem to me all the uses of this world.[2]

And the Psalmist:

> Ye are gods, but ye shall die like men.

This consciousness of death, finititude, produces great acts of heroism, is a spur to the moral sense. It can also stir in ordinary folk the spirit of compassion as we see that we are all faced with the same destiny. St Luke's account of the penitent thief's words to the impenitent: 'Dost not thou fear God, seeing thou art in the same condemnation.' Death, the great leveller.

We fear death as an end of our deepest relationships. Yet this fear is not unproductive when it makes us attend to those relationships, "to be kindly affectioned one to another." Because I am not here for ever, then I must make sure that I use the precious time rightly and well. It is also in this sense that death is the origin of morality. There needs to be no judgement seat: death is the final reckoning. It is against this absolute that all our actions are judged – that is, judged by our own conscience. In this noble solidarity there is the spring of moral action, of goodness, and a sort of consolation.

And it works in the other direction. If the consciousness of death produces a solidarity with others – "We die with the dying" – which issues in more compassionate behaviour, then the compassionate behaviour helps us face death with a clearer conscience: "We are born with the dead." As we noticed in the chapter on bereavement, guilt is a large part of death's malign influence, and the pains attached to it. That is the psychological meaning of the saying, "The sting of death is sin." The Epistle of St John is the best declaration on the psychology of moral feelings and the fear of death. The antidote to fear is virtue. For Christian thought, virtue is summed up in the word love (*agapē*). And, as St John says, "Perfect love casts our fear."

The injunction to do good so that you may enjoy eternal life, can be seen on the here and now psychological level as meaning that a moral life dispels the fear of death. The opposite is also true: we are aware of our failure to live a moral life, and so our apprehension at the prospect of death is increased. The psychology of all this is, as usual, well-treated by the gospels: if we think we are living a moral life, we are probably hypocrites. "And he spake this parable to certain that thought themselves righteous and despised others." And St Paul repeats and repeats the fact, "None is righteous, no, not one."

Since "the wages of sin is death" how then do we sinners cope? Perfect love may cast out fear, but what of us who do not have perfect love? How to face the absolute assize of death knowing our imperfection? For the fear of death is always mixed with the sense of guilt. If we cannot justify ourselves, how shall we be justified? The New Testament wrestles with all these psychological paradoxes and produces the answer, Grace. It is a kind of grace . . . And such grace as we experience is mediated by those who love us. This means that they do not in fact treat us as if we were broken, imperfect, niggardly; but that, knowing us, they yet love us and care for us.

It is a kind of transcending sign: when we experience what it is to be loved, we are lifted almost as it were above life and death into a different spiritual and emotional dimension. It is part of the meaning of "the pearl of great price" for which we would give everything – because love, being loved, is everything and we know it. Again and again we return to the substance of the epic drama, which is love and death; to Freud who gave us the psychological dynamics of those two realities: Eros and Thanatos. They are the two poles, the governing realities, the spiritual and psychological ultimate criteria. They are in some ways opposites, but in other ways very close. So that, in art, and particularly in Romantic art and music, love and death are twins: to employ a Romantic phrase, love and death are lovers.

There is the *Liebestod*. There is the highest form of drama, the tragedy, in which love and death are always the main themes. Epic and biblical poetry presents the same love-death syzygy: David's lament for the beloved Jonathan. "Rachel, weeping for her children and would not be comforted, because they are not."

Love, while it lasts, can assuage the fear of death. Death and the inevitability of it adds poignancy to love. Even the suicide pact is the dark side of the lover's tryst. Love and death share their affinity because they are each overriding; nothing is greater in the mind of the lover than his love; nothing can gainsay death. And so there is the terrifying ambiguity in the truth that love can lift us above the fear of death while it must also be finally subject to death's inevitability.

Another part of the fear of death is the intensity of life.

You look at the full green trees on a warm summer's day, or else at the waves beating under the cliff; and the power of the experience is an amalgamation of joy and woe. You want to be able to capture the scene, the moment and preserve it. But you cannot. You may look, now. But the picture finally transcends you. Enjoy the ecstatic glance for, as you are only too well aware, you cannot possess the scene and it will remain when you have gone. Hardy knew this:

> When the Present has latched its postern behind my
>   tremulous stay,
> And the May month flaps its glad green leaves like
>   wings,
> Delicate-filmed as new-spun silk, will the neighbours
>   say,
> "He was a man who used to notice such things"?[3]

The sharpness of our perception of the world, the depth of our feelings about it, coupled with the knowledge of our own finiteness: these things add to the melancholy power of death. But perhaps a kind of reconciliation is possible.

The composer Gustav Mahler lived his whole life under the shadow of death. Each one of his ten symphonies is an attempt to answer the question, in his own words: "Why do we live? Why do we suffer? Is this just a horrible dream? We must answer these questions if we are to go on living. We must answer them if we are only to go on dying."

The answers he was looking for were not theoretical, "explanations" of "the meaning of life" or "proofs" of an afterlife. For reasons we have already noticed, theories and explanations do not, however exalted they might be, assuage our fear of death. This is because life itself is much nearer to us than any theory or explanation. Our relationship with life, with the world, is personal and intimate. When we look at those full green trees on the warm summer day, we feel that in a sense the scene is *ours*. Our own back garden. "He was a man who used to notice such things." We left the world of the womb traumatically to make this world our home. We are as attached to it as to the womb. Between womb and tomb this third attachment. This world is our natural element and we are not distinct from it.

The fact that we can talk about the world, propositionalize it, gives rise to the delusion that we are somehow separate from it or above it. When this mood is on us, we may feel arrogantly superior to the natural world, because we can describe and define it, measure it, put it in its place. Or else we may feel a sense of alienation and not belonging. This is the price we pay for having become creatures who use an advanced language.

But the feeling of separateness is a delusion. We are part of the world, "of the earth, earthy". Its sounds and sights fill our senses. Its air fills our lungs. Its produce fills our bellies. We do not measure the world in any intimate sense, but the world has the measure of us. It is this closeness to the earth which makes the prospect of death frightening, traumatic. The similarities with the womb are close: we speak affectionately of Mother Earth. Without our mother, where shall we be? Knowing that we shall one day be without her, how do we cope now?

A time-honoured way is to pay her much attention. The love of nature, the care of a garden. Even, in England, the everlasting talk about the weather! Coping with our fear of death means getting closer to the earth and to nature, and not retreating from them. "God made the country, man made the town." It is a general truth that countryfolk are less fearful of death than townsfolk. The necessary acceptance that death is natural is more likely to develop in the countryside. And that is another reason to regret the urbanization of our country scene and village life by the motorcar, mass communication and all the habits of thought which prevail in the towns. When urban living makes natural life and awareness more distant, it also removes from us the naturalness of death and undermines nature's own way of helping us cope with the inevitable. Some time spent, then, in contact with nature, the earth, and in contemplation of it, is a comfort in the face of death which is not available from any other source. An acquaintance with the natural life-cycle is naturally comforting – even if it only extends to noticing spring's buds and autumn's embers. It is possible to live in the city, with our fluorescent light and air-conditioning, and hardly know whether it is day or night, let alone summer or winter. No wonder the event of death seems so alien and hostile in such an environment.

But to return to Mahler's desperate questions. In his early symphonies he tried to work out answers to these questions by introducing various sorts of death-defying motifs. In the first symphony – in which there is an evocation of his brother who died when Mahler was fifteen – he pits against death the idea of the hero. The symphony was originally called "The Titan". The second symphony, "The Resurrection" affirms the afterlife to assuage our fear of death. It is worth noting in passing, though, that it did convince an old lady whom Mahler met on a railway platform in Russia. She asked him to tell her what heaven is like. She said that anyone who could compose a work like the second symphony must know all about it. I suppose Mahler might have replied, "Listen to the music!"

In nearly all his work, Mahler fights against death. He

uses Love (symphony number three) and, Childhood Evocations (number four). In the sixth he invokes Tragedy in a work of horror and desolation in which he seems to say that his desparate questions do not have any answers. In the eighth he calls on Creativity in the Person of the Holy Spirit and also on *Das Ewig Weibliche* – the Romantic femininity of Goethe's *Faust*.

Only in the ninth symphony and in *Das Lied von der Erde* (The Song of the Earth) Mahler ceases to call up Titans and resurrections and the rest to answer his spiritual questions about death: instead, he comes to something approaching an acceptance of it. And this acceptance of death partly involves an acceptance of himself as part of nature. At the end of *Der Abschied* (The Farewell) which is the last movement of *Das Lied*, Mahler writes: "Where am I going? I go now to the mountains. I seek peace for my lonely heart. I wander to my homeland, my abode. I will never roam in the distance. My heart is quiet and awaits its hour! Everywhere the good earth once more greens and blossoms into spring. Everywhere, forever, distant spaces shine light blue! Forever . . . forever!"

In order to get the full flavour of this acceptance, which, however, is full of rich nostalgia and love of natural things, there is no substitute for listening to the words and music together as they bring *Der Abschied* to its powerful and tender conclusion. Here is a sound picture of a man who has, for his whole lifetime, felt so agonizingly the reality of death, but who now effects a reconciliation with death through an expressed evocation and love of life – the life of earth and sky.

If we attend to living nature we shall not suffer the anxiety which is a living death. But it is not just a case of nature itself; art, poetry and music do not give us nature at second-hand, but a distillation of its spirit. Moreover, because art requires an artist, it also presents us with a powerfully felt union between the human agent and the world of nature. Great art encapsulates nature for us and reveals our true relationship with it. Mahler's late works do this overwhelmingly.

To describe better this relationship between art and nature, Mahler's own words to his wife Alma when she came out to visit him at his composer's hut in the hills: "No need to look at the hills – I've composed them all already!"

The same indestructible partnership between art and the world of mortal experience, between the creative mind and the substance of the natural, physical world, can be felt in Mahler's *Der Einsame im Herbst* (The Lonely Man in Autumn) – another part of *Das Lied*:

> A blue autumn mist hovers over the lake;
> All the grass-blades are striped with frost;
> One would think an artist had strewn jade-dust
> Over the delicate blossoms.

> My heart is weary. My little lamp
> Went out with a hiss, reminding me of sleep.
> I am coming to you, beloved resting-place!
> Yes, give me peace! I need to be refreshed!

> I weep much in my loneliness;
> Autumn has lasted too long in my heart.
> Sun of love, will you never shine again,
> And gently dry my bitter tears?

Nature is a comfort for us because we are part of it and we cannot but describe ourselves in the natural terms which it offers us. So Wordsworth wanders lonely . . . "as a cloud". Our hope and desperation is expressed in such

143

as, "Every cloud has a silver lining." We are "tempest tossed" and "adrift". If we are depressed, we are "drowning". If elated, "on the heights". Even popular songs express the felt, emotional link between human experience and the natural order: "Nothing but blue skies from now on." Such phrases as "The sea of faith", "The winter of our discontent" and "The dark night of the soul".

These phrases and images, and ten thousand like them, are proof – if proof were needed – that our lives are bound up with the life of nature. We are incarnated into a world of sense and feelings, a tangible world which houses our own personal reality. When we rejoice, we take its food and wine. When we need comfort, we turn to Mother Earth also. If we can feel that we are a part of a creation, an order, which is greater than ourselves, then perhaps we can, like Mahler in *Das Lied*, feel not afraid because we shall soon be sundered from it, but at peace because we know that we are a part of something which will endure when we have gone. The best help in coping with the fact of our own death is Mother Nature. If we adopt the opposite of the technological mentality which only desires to subdue nature in the interests of prolonging, and rendering more comfortable, human life, and, instead of trying to force our revisions upon the natural world, we learn a little acceptance of things as they are – to be formed by what has formed us – then we shall derive much comfort in the face of the deathly fear: because we shall realize that we are a part of something that is real, beautiful and enduring.

> I took my love to the sea, that night;
> The waves like silver thread under the moon . . .[4]

These fragments have I shored against my ruins.[5]

The natural world, fresh, green-budded, springlike – or misty, mellow, turning auburn and red between the encroaching frosts – lays upon us a creative nostalgia. It is a world of sights and scents. Of sounds. A real, felt world in which we are incarnated and from which we can never really depart. For, despite all our computers and electronic sophistications we are "solid flesh" and "mortal coils". The birds sing in the deep wood. And the sun comes out, hot on your face. "And the children in the apple tree."

All these things are real, not abstractions; not ideas or theories. And so we can trust them . . . if I may use the phrase, bury ourselves in them. In the days before our technological urbanity our burial in the earth was a sign and (I will dare say it!) an *underwriting* of these things. In the midst of life we are in death. And, we may add, in the midst of death we are in life. Nature knows these as two aspects of the same indivisible reality.

Closeness to the natural world, and the powerful memories which this creates, is the deepest consolation.

> . . . mixing
> Memory and desire, stirring
> Dull roots with spring rain.[6]

There is nowhere else to go but to the earth, nowhere more sustaining. The earth is what we know, what has made us. It is the sum and composite of all our experiences and relationships – the creator of our language, for our language consists firstly of names of things on earth. If we wish to know of heaven and heavenly things, we must first learn of the earth. "The good earth", as Mahler says, will not let us down when we need consoling. And part of the meaning of "the earth" is all the others who have lived on it, including especially those, like Mahler and the great poets and musicians, artists, who have *presented* the earth to us by their forms of artistic expression. This whole earthly experience, recorded in language, pictures and musical sounds, is the sum of what we mean by "the earth" and our lives in it together. Solidarity. "No man is an island." Charity. Warmheartedness.

So, turning to our earth, we learn that there is nothing to fear, for there is nothing that is not given by our experience of the earth. Nothing comes out of nothing. Our earth is not an impersonal vastness, which is what the town suggests; it is a warmhearted intimacy – disturbed in the storm and calm on the summer breeze – which belongs to us all and which nothing can take away from us.

Moreover, we do not even have to rely on direct experience and strenuous interpretation of it for the whole time. Art, building on the world, distils it for us. We are compassed about by so great a cloud of witnesses: all the poets and painters, Mahler, Shakespeare, Van Gogh. "We have art so that we do not die of the truth," said Nietzsche. But his remark is unnecessarily cynical. Art *is* the truth. Otherwise its poignancy and loveliness would not move us. There are things we can trust.

In the artist, then, the creative urge is a war on death, an attempt to produce something that will survive his own death. This is why great artists are sometimes referred to as "immortals" and their work as "timeless". They are not immortal, though. And even the most original of works belongs to its time, its era. Moreover, it is the sharpness in his sensation or apprehension of death which spurs the artist to produce something that will transcend death. The artist is nothing other than the person who speaks our human language, our humanity then, at the highest (or we may say the deepest) level. So the artist is a sort of priest. What Shakespeare has done for us, what Mozart has done, we cannot do for ourselves.

Art is a consolation because the artist articulates the depths for us. We totter about, more or less blindly, feeling our way in the presence of the archetypal feelings of birth and death: the artist visits those realms and creates something out of them which says what we want to say, but says it more clearly, more directly. The consolation is also a reconciliation. If you listen to the Mozart *Requiem*, there is the orchestration of death, but not of death only; there is Mozart putting death in its place. That someone could write so accurately, so comprehendingly, about even *this* gives us hope. Death has no dominion over him. If the resurrection ever finds a visible sign in this world, it is in the mystery by which art turns death into life, destruction and entropy into vitality, a new creation. It is not an accident that some of the most beautiful pictures are of the crucifixion.

So we can go to art and find consolation and freedom from the fear of death, because in art we see death transcended. This does not directly answer metaphysical questions, such as the ones over which Mahler agonized, "Why do we live? Why do we suffer?" The move is more indirect: by portraying the questions themselves – the crucified Christ, for instance – art insists that these questions have meaning. And that says that we have meaning. And that is the consolation in the face of death, for the fear of death is mainly the fear of ultimate meaninglessness. Mahler put it the other way round: "We must answer these questions if we are only to continue *dying*." The creative portrayal of our dying is what answers the unanswerable questions. It may be expressed

aphoristically: someone said that the Allegri *Miserere* is
"The short proof of the existence of God". This was not
meant as a logical solution to an imponderable
metaphysical question. It is itself something like a work
of art. "The short proof of the existence of God" – what
did he mean, whoever said those words? He meant, I
suggest, to affirm being and wellbeing in the face of what
terrifies us. He meant what Eliot and Mother Julian
meant:

> All shall be well and
> All manner of thing shall be well.

The Allegri made him feel that to be true in a way that
goes beyond mere speculation about gods and eternal life;
made him know it. And, in a world that is truly incarnated
– and in a secular age perhaps art is the only such world
– the word "know" has more than a mental, propositional
connotation: "Adam knew his wife Eve, and she
conceived and bare Cain . . ."

* * *

We combat the fear of death, then, by turning to the
natural world and by realizing how death itself is
transcended in art, music and literature. Both the cycle
of nature and the creativity in all true artistic expression
give the lie to the fear that the world and we are
meaningless. Our meaning may be, as Sophocles and
Shakespeare suggest, a tragic meaning; nonetheless, we
are not *for nothing*. Mere duration does not confer
meaning. The world is not senseless or malign just
because we do not live forever.

Nature and art are not our only comforts. There is
morality and there is work.

The morally encouraging aspect of death arises directly out of the horror of it: namely that we are conscious of our eventual death, but we can do nothing about it. This gives us, in certain circumstances, a moral superiority over the brute fact of death. We can, in war for instance or in other situations which call for sacrifice, give our lives on behalf of others. This is the ethical answer to the fear of death. We can, in full knowledge of what we do, lay down our lives for our friends and our countrymen. This gives us the ascendancy. Death and the fear of death are great, but the human spirit is greater. When, on the Antarctic expedition, Captain Oates walked out into the blizzard as the only means to save his friends, he died: but that sort of heroic death is a moral victory over death. It shows the glory of man. It is there in war and acts of rescue under fire in no man's land. It is there in the lifeboat and the fire-engine; in every act of humane unselfishness where lives are risked and often lost. This moral victory over death consists in one thing: it shows that there is something more important even than death. Acts of courage and self-sacrifice put death in its place, and that is what is meant by our moral victory over death. "Greater love hath no man than this, that he lay down his life for his friends."

And it is a real victory. Death is, after all, a nothing. It is the opposite of life. It is not (as we have seen) eternal, because in death there is no such thing as time. Death is non-being, nothing. Life is all. The fact that human beings are capable of self-sacrifice shows the triumph of life over death. *That* we die is a banality; *how* we die defines us as human.

It follows from this that not only the vast heroic gesture of self-sacrifice, but also every little act of self-giving, is a triumph of life over death. For every moral choice and action, because it is real choice involving real action, affirms the meaning and dignity of life. We are not in blind thrall to supernatural forces and the final inevitability of death. We can act and choose. This fact gives us the moral supremacy over death. Thus the life well lived is the answer to death and all its fears, and is the triumph over it. This much is seen in the life and death of Christ. He is the example for every man who values moral action – how we actually live and die – above the mere eventuality of death. To have human values which are higher, more personally important, than death and the fear of death is what puts death in its place, helps us cope with it.

The other antidote to the fear of death is work. For work, something actually done, achieved, is a kind of immortality. Death can do nothing. Death is only the great black impotence. Any work in which we are involved, knowing that our work must one day cease, is an act of heroism. We do something. We build a bridge or write a poem. We dig the garden or invent the bicycle. What we have done has really been done. Mortal man, conscious of his finite nature, can still do something significant: in Samuel Beckett's words, "Leave a stain on the silence".

Our work, whatever it is, is the affirmation of life in the face of death. It is also a great reliever of anxiety. Work done gives a sense of satisfaction, achievement. Thomas Carlyle, depressed about the fact of death and the fear of meaninglessness, said, "Work while it is yet light, for the night cometh wherein no man can work." A stain on the silence. Death, for all its terrors, can alter nothing. It is a bald negativity. Life and work significantly alter and reshape the world. This is why work assuages the fear of death.

Mahler – he of the impossible questions – also found this to be true. Near the end of his life he said, "When I am composing, I feel I have the answers to all these questions; or rather, I feel they are not questions at all." It does not matter what our work is. But what we do defines who we are. In this sense, our work *is* our nature, our identity. Death is mere nothing, oblivion, anonymity. Work is exactly the opposite: it is intelligence, consciousness and individuality. Work of the highest order demonstrates this truth. Think of a Stradivarius violin or a Beethoven symphony, a novel by George Eliot or a painting by Leonardo. What is the black, timeless anonymity of death beside these things? Those works having been done, death does not matter. Mozart – died in 1791 – Mozart lives! I can prove it by walking to the gramophone. A stain on the silence.

*   *   *

There is, at the last, another word to be said about death. We do not only fear it; we are also attracted by it. It has, as you might say, a fatal fascination. Else why all the ghoulish films and children's games of murder most foul? There is a part of us which is "half in love with easeful death".

Freud identified a life-principle in us, but also, especially in his later work, something like a death-wish. There is nothing necessarily morbid about this. Death is the natural end to life, so why should there not be a part of us which tends towards it, longs for it sometimes? There is the cry for deliverance which may also be applied to death – the deliverance from life: "How long, O Lord, how long?"

Death itself need not be feared. But Socrates said, "The unexamined life is not worth living." To this we might add that the unreconciled death is the only thing to fear.

If nature, art, work, love, charity and grace can all help us towards an acceptance of death, then it has to be said that there are, alas, people who leave this life as they entered it – kicking and screaming, as it were. This is the psychological meaning of Jesus' saying about not fearing death but the need to fear being cast into hell. Psychologically speaking, the fear and terror of death – the unreconciled death – *is* hell. Grace makes it possible for everyone to achieve a reconciled death and a calm acceptance of it: but it has to be admitted that in some cases this calm reconciliation does not come. Unfortunately, not every story has a happy ending.

But the naturalness of death can be made to work for us, assuaging our fear. Freud and Jung speak of this. So does Keats. And Swinburne looked forward to death as a return to a sort of metaphorical paradise garden, *The Garden of Proserpine* (death):

> From too much love of living,
> From hope and fear set free,
> We thank with brief thanksgiving,
> Whatever gods may be
> That no man lives for ever,
> That dead men rise up never;
> That even the weariest river
> Winds somewhere safe to sea.[7]

Let it be a help and consolation to see death not always as The Last Enemy but as The Final Resting Place. "I will lay me down in peace and take my rest." "There is a time to live and a time to die." Nothing morbid or gloomy about that: it is all part of the one natural whole.

The mystical teachers knew that death can be kind, that it can be the darkness, too, which leads to God. St Francis:

> ... thou most kind and gentle death,
> Waiting to hush our latest breath.[8]

It is the seed cast into the ground which burgeons forth. But this, as St Paul said, is a mystery which we cannot penetrate. At the beginning of this chapter I tried to describe the linguistic and philosophical impossibility of talking meaningfully about any afterlife or future state.

But I return finally to the Bible and the Prayer Book, and their achievement in telling the truth about human beings and our life on this earth. Those books tell us that we are sinners, "vile bodies", "worms destroy this body," "ashes to ashes, dust to dust", and so on. The Bible does not spare reality – only, as we saw earlier, our euphemisms about life and death do.

The greatest and most reassuring comfort for me is in the Bible's psychological and spiritual realism. There is no lessening of the mystery, no way of lifting the veil and discovering what eternal life and heaven mean. But I find it impossible to doubt that the Bible and the Prayer Book – having got everything else right – should somehow falter and fall into mere sentimentality when it comes to the resurrection.

The language is elusive, not literal. But it is there, like the rest of the words about death and sin:

> Our Lord Jesus Christ; who shall change our vile body, that it may be like unto his glorious body.

> ... whosoever liveth and believeth in me shall never die.

> ... in my flesh shall I see God: whom I shall see for myself, and mine eyes shall behold, and not another.

All those words come from *The Burial of the Dead*, a

remarkable composition which has attracted the entirely unjustifiable accusation that it is morbid.

And this is how that service ends:

Come ye blessed children of my Father, receive the kingdom prepared for you from the beginning of the world: Grant this, we beseech thee, O merciful Father, through Jesus Christ, our Mediator and Redeemer.

AMEN

It is the way we end, too.

NOTES

CHAPTER 1

1 T. S. Eliot: "Four Quartets" (Faber & Faber)
2 W. Shakespeare: *Julius Caesar*, II. ii. 30
3 1 John 3:2
4 W. Shakespeare: *Hamlet*, III. i. 66
5 T. Stoppard: *Rosencrantz and Guildenstern are Dead* (Faber & Faber, 1967)
6 W. Shakespeare: *Macbeth*, V. v. 26
7 W. Shakespeare: *Cymbeline*, IV. ii. 262
8 T. S. Eliot "Four Quartets" (Faber & Faber)

CHAPTER 2

1 T. S. Eliot: "Ash Wednesday" (Faber & Faber)
2 T. S. Eliot: "Four Quartets" (Faber & Faber)
3 Mother Julian of Norwich: *Revelations of Divine Love*, Ch. xxvii
4 N. Malcolm: *Wittgenstein: A Memoir* (Routledge & Kegan Paul)
5 1 Corinthians 15:47

CHAPTER 3

1 Figures for 1988, provided by the City of York Crematorium

CHAPTER 4

1 W. Shakespeare: *The Tempest*, IV. i. 156
2 T. S. Eliot: "Four Quartets" (Faber & Faber)
3 I. Watts: "When I Survey the Wondrous Cross"

CHAPTER 5

1 Descartes's conclusion was later refuted by Wittgenstein: see *Philosphical Investigations*, paras 243–315
2 W. Shakespeare: *Hamlet*, III. i. 56
3 Ibid. III. i. 61
4 Ibid. III. i. 65
5 A. Alvarez: *The Savage God* (Weidenfeld and Nicolson)
6 W. Shakespeare: *Hamlet*, III. i. 89
7 Ibid. II. ii. (316)
8 Ibid. II. ii. (259)
9 W. Blake: *Notebooks*
10 T. S. Eliot: "Four Quartets" (Faber & Faber)
11 F. M. Dostoevsky: *Diary of a Writer* (Penguin)
12 F. W. Nietzsche: *Beyond Good and Evil*
13 A. Schopenhauer: "On Suicide", *Essays and Aphorisms* (Penguin)
14 A. Schopenhauer: "The Indestructibility of Being", *Essays and Aphorisms* (Penguin)
15 A. Alvarez: *The Savage God* (Weidenfeld and Nicolson)
16 E. Pound: "Mr Housman's Message", *Collected Short Poems* (Faber & Faber)
17 V. Scannell: "Felo de Se", *New and Collected Poems* (Robson Books)
18 1 John 4:10
19 W. Blake: "The Divine Image"
20 T. S. Eliot: *The Cocktail Party* (Faber & Faber)
21 T. S. Eliot: "Four Quartets" (Faber & Faber)

CHAPTER 6

1 J. Donne: *Holy Sonnets*, VII
2 W. Shakespeare: *Hamlet* I. ii. 133
3 T. Hardy: *Afterwards*
4 P. Mullen: "Loss"
5 T. S. Eliot: "The Waste Land" (Faber & Faber)
6 Ibid.
7 A. C. Swinburne: "The Garden of Proserpine"
8 W. H. Draper: Hymn based on St Francis of Assisi's "Canticle of the Sun"

Also available in Fount Paperbacks

The Holy Spirit
BILLY GRAHAM

'This is far and away Graham's best book. It bears the stamp of someone who has seen everything, and then has worked painstakingly and carefully in making his own assessment . . . The Christian world will be reading it for many years to come.'

Richard Bewes,
Church of England Newspaper

To Live Again
CATHERINE MARSHALL

The moving story of one woman's heart-rending grief and of her long hard struggle to rediscovery of herself, of life, of hope.

A Man Called Peter
CATHERINE MARSHALL

The story of a brilliantly successful minister and of a dynamic personality. Told by his wife, it is also the story of their life together; a record of love and faith that has few equals in real life.

The Prayers of Peter Marshall
CATHERINE MARSHALL

'This is a truly wonderful book, for these prayers are a man speaking to God – and speaking in a way that involves listening for an answer.'

British Weekly

Also available in Fount Paperbacks

BOOKS BY C. S. LEWIS

The Abolition of Man

'It is the most perfectly reasoned defence of Natural Law (Morality) I have ever seen, or believe to exist.'

Walter Hooper

Mere Christianity

'He has a quite unique power for making theology an attractive, exciting and fascinating quest.'

Times Literary Supplement

God in the Dock

'This little book . . . consists of some brilliant pieces . . . This is just the kind of book to place into the hands of an intellectual doubter . . . It has been an unalloyed pleasure to read.'

Marcus Beverley, Christian Herald

The Great Divorce

'Mr Lewis has a rare talent for expressing spiritual truth in fresh and striking imagery and with uncanny acumen . . . it contains many flashes of deep insight and exposures of popular fallacies.'

Church Times

Fount Paperbacks

Fount is one of the leading paperback publishers of religious books and below are some of its recent titles.

- ☐ FRIENDSHIP WITH GOD David Hope £2.95
- ☐ THE DARK FACE OF REALITY Martin Israel £2.95
- ☐ LIVING WITH CONTRADICTION Esther de Waal £2.95
- ☐ FROM EAST TO WEST Brigid Marlin £3.95
- ☐ GUIDE TO THE HERE AND HEREAFTER
                              Lionel Blue/Jonathan Magonet £4.50
- ☐ CHRISTIAN ENGLAND (1 Vol) David Edwards £10.95
- ☐ MASTERING SADHANA Carlos Valles £3.95
- ☐ THE GREAT GOD ROBBERY George Carey £2.95
- ☐ CALLED TO ACTION Fran Beckett £2.95
- ☐ TENSIONS Harry Williams £2.50
- ☐ CONVERSION Malcolm Muggeridge £2.95
- ☐ INVISIBLE NETWORK Frank Wright £2.95
- ☐ THE DANCE OF LOVE Stephen Verney £3.95
- ☐ THANK YOU, PADRE Joan Clifford £2.50
- ☐ LIGHT AND LIFE Grazyna Sikorska £2.95
- ☐ CELEBRATION Margaret Spufford £2.95
- ☐ GOODNIGHT LORD Georgette Butcher £2.95
- ☐ GROWING OLDER Una Kroll £2.95

All Fount Paperbacks are available at your bookshop or newsagent, or they can be ordered by post from Fount Paperbacks, Cash Sales Department, G.P.O. Box 29, Douglas, Isle of Man. Please send purchase price plus 22p per book, maximum postage £3. Customers outside the UK send purchase price, plus 22p per book. Cheque, postal order or money order. No currency.

NAME (Block letters) _____

ADDRESS_____

_____

_____